I0058686

# SEVEN FIGURE BLUEPRINTS

A Proven System For Creating Million Dollar Digital Marketing Campaigns.

Richard Legg

The information in this book was correct at the time of publication, but the author does not assume any liability for loss or damage caused by errors or omissions. Revised edition. First edition previously published as Hidden Profits. All information is provided for general informational and educational purposes only.



www.SevenFigureBlueprints.com

# CONTENTS

# INTRODUCTION: THE NEED TO EVOLVE

On December 17, 1903, brothers Orville and Wilbur Wright became the first people to successfully complete a powered flight with an aircraft. The flight only lasted 12 seconds and covered just over 120 feet, but it would change the course of human history.

This flight was the culmination of seven years of hard work and over 700 previous tests with unpowered gliders. When it came time to build a powered craft, they couldn't find an automobile engine that was powerful enough, or light enough, for their needs. So in true entrepreneurial spirit they built their own.

As their aircraft took to the skies on that December morning, all of their determination, experimentation, and hard work finally paid off.

More than 100 years later, that simple plane piloted by Orville is unrecognizable compared to the aircraft of today. We now fly around the world, tens of thousands of feet in the sky, at hundreds of miles an hour. Cabins carry hundreds of people in relative comfort. Furthermore, these planes can fly almost unaided for hours at a time.

So what does this have to do with getting more profit from your business?

Simple. If you have an existing business already, you've traveled a similar path to the Wright brothers. Getting a business “off the ground” has many similarities to getting that first plane airborne. It’s the result of countless hours of effort, determination, and often sacrifice.

But that is usually where the similarity ends. After Orville and Wilbur’s successful flight of just 120 feet, nobody ever said, “Okay, great. We’ve got this flying thing down,” and left it at that. The aviation world has evolved, though unfortunately, many businesses do not.

Far too many business owners get so caught up ‘in’ their business that they’re unable to work ‘on’ their business and improve it.

Instead of building a more powerful engine to go further or faster, many business owners simply try to add a bigger fuel tank to their existing small engine.

A business needs to improve, grow, and evolve in order to survive. If the aviation world never evolved, some other mode of transport would have overtaken it.

In business there is always a way to improve. The difficult part is usually knowing *what* to improve.

As a business owner, it’s often difficult to step back and slow down or change the direction of your business. Sometimes you don’t even know which direction is best.

To have the best chance of growing your business, you need to look at the direction your business is taking sooner rather than later. Abraham Lincoln once said, “Give me six hours to chop down a tree and I will spend the first four sharpening the axe.” If you put in the effort to prepare now, it will be easier for you to execute later.

With this book you’ll be able to use my proven methods for doubling your business in the easiest way possible. These are the same methods I use to build seven figure digital marketing campaigns for myself and clients. If you’re willing to put in a little effort, I’ll show you how to extract hidden revenue from your business that you didn't know existed.

The key with this approach is that we're not looking to go from zero to 100 miles an hour in a few seconds. Just like in the aviation world, it has taken time to go from being able to fly 120 feet, to being able to fly thousands of miles at a time.

These principles will show you how to constantly iterate and improve on a small scale. That way you're always moving forward and building on the foundation you lay. It may be slow to start out, but with constant forward motion, those little steps will have a profound impact over time.

If you're looking to grow your business, you may be asking yourself, why don't we just spend more on advertising or hire more people? Those are valid questions, and they can be valid approaches. However, my method generates fast results for your business with minimal outlay in time and money.

Rather than encouraging you to blindly spend more and more money on marketing, I'll teach you my methods for unlocking hidden revenue sources that already exist within your current business, as well as adding new ones. I'll guide you through the steps you need to attract more visitors, generate more customers, and increase revenue without having to spend any more on marketing.

Focus on using assets that you already have first, instead of trying to build new revenue streams, and you'll see results much quicker.

Once you've unlocked those hidden revenue sources within your business, there's nothing to stop you from spending more money on advertising later or building in new income streams.

With a business that runs more efficiently, any money spent on advertising has a much greater chance of yielding a positive return.

Once you know that your current business generates more customers and more revenue per customer, you can afford to spend more on advertising. You'll grow your business even further while getting bigger profits.

This method doesn't have to be time or labor intensive. My goal is to have you make small, incremental changes that perform just that little bit better each day, week, or month. Over time, those results are compounded into something substantial.

# PREFACE: SLOW AND STEADY WINS THE RACE. LITERALLY.

The methodology behind this process is the aggregation of marginal gains. Put simply, this is a philosophy for making many small improvements that together compound into large gains.

I've divided this book into sections that follow those principles and give you a clear path to follow.

The concept of aggregation of marginal gains was used heavily by Sir Dave Brailsford, a performance director hired by the Team Sky cycling team to take Britain to a Tour de France win. His method was to break down the sport of cycling and improve each area by just 1%.

That included not only the physical act of riding the bike, but all aspects of the athlete's life. His belief was that improving each aspect by a small amount would result in a large overall gain.

Sir Dave started by optimizing the obvious things, such as training programs, nutrition, etc., but the process went much deeper than that.

For example, in the trucks transporting the bikes, he noticed that dust and dirt would often accumulate and stick to the bikes. That would reduce aerodynamic efficiency, even if only on a tiny scale. By painting the floors of the trucks a bright white color, they were able to keep them clean and minimize the impact of transportation.

When the athletes traveled with the pillows they found most comfortable, they were able to get a better night's rest. By learning about the best way to thoroughly wash their hands, they were able to minimize infections and illnesses.

The belief was that if it was possible to execute this strategy, then they would be able to win the Tour de France within five years. In fact, it took only three years, with Sir Bradley Wiggins winning in 2012.

At the same time, Brailsford coached the British cycling team for the Summer Olympics in 2012. Following the same methodology, the Team GB cycling team went on to win 70% of all the gold medals they competed for in those games. The following year, in 2013, Team Sky won the Tour de France again.

So the process of looking for tiny, one-percent improvements is something that's simple to follow. It's also relatively easy to implement, but the potential gains should not be underestimated. Go slow, go steady, and win that race.

Another reason this process works well is that you're focusing on something that is already working. While you can use the principles to start a new business for the best possible chance of success, it's going to provide bigger gains if you already have some momentum.

A lot of business owners reach a certain point where they seem to plateau in terms of their results. They can't get greater results without a disproportionate amount of effort. In many cases, they feel the only way to move forward is to start a whole new other business.

However, starting something from scratch requires a huge amount of effort, which is not the most efficient path to take.

If you've ever tried to push a car that's broken down, you'll know that 90% of your effort goes into getting over the initial inertia and moving that first inch. Once the car is moving and has some momentum, it's much easier to keep it moving.

It's the same with business. If you already have momentum with something, even if it feels like the acceleration has stalled, it's better to try and get that moving faster rather than putting on the brakes and trying to get something else started from a standstill.

## Small Changes, Big Results

One of the reasons it's important to look for small, marginal gains is that success breeds enthusiasm. I get really excited about split test results – although that may just be the physics nerd in me coming out. But any positive result, no matter how small, is something that keeps you motivated.

By making your goal bigger, the rewards will be bigger too; however, it becomes difficult to maintain that motivation.

Going for a 100% improvement is not impossible. With the right approach and dedication you will get improvements of 20, 30, 40, or 50%, which are all significant improvements.

But if your goal is 100% every time, you're going to be missing your goal most of the time, even if you're constantly improving. The result is that you end up losing motivation and momentum.

It's also important to realize that with lots of these small individual improvements, the effects will compound themselves. Albert Einstein supposedly once said that the most powerful force in the universe is compound interest.

## The Power of Compounding

You might be familiar with the story of how doubling a penny every day for 30 days results in a total of over five million dollars. This is an extreme example, but it shows the power of compounding.

When applying that to business, the way to approach it is to break down your business into several key areas and look for the specific parts you can leverage to produce gains.

I call these key areas "profit multipliers". The effects of each will compound on the others to produce something that is greater than their individual parts.

In this book we'll cover eight key profit multiplier areas in your business. They are:

- People
- Prospects
- Purchases
- Products
- Pricing
- Persistence
- Profitability
- Productivity

Your goal will be to achieve just a 10% increase in each area. Doing that at a minimum will double your business.

To demonstrate the power of compounding, consider these examples:

- A 10% increase in eight areas is not 80%, but actually 114%.
- A 25% increase in eight areas is not 200%, but 496%.
- A 50% increase in eight areas is not 400%, but 2,460%.

In other words, the bigger the increase, the larger the compounding effect is.

It's easy to fall into the trap of going for those big gains, but again you'll find they quickly become too big to be attainable. The result is that you lose momentum.

So with just a 10% increase to focus on, the goal is achievable.

In fact, just a 1% increase per month in eight areas would give you a 159% increase after 12 months.

To put that into context, if you started off with a business today making $100,000, improving each area just 1% per month would give you a business generating over $250,000 in 12 months' time – without you having to spend any more on advertising.

Making a 1% improvement should be more than possible. Even if you only improved nine months out of 12, you'd still double your business by year end.

But before you start working on the eight profit multipliers, there's something else to consider.

Preparation.

For the process to work correctly, you need to make sure you're building on a solid foundation and moving in the right direction.

## Consideration #1: Know Where You're Going, but Also Where You've Been

Probably the most important element of this whole experience will be that you need to be able to track accurately. If you want to get from A to B, it's important to know not only where B is, but also where A is.

Before you make any improvements, you need to have a really good understanding of where your business is currently. You'll want to analyze what is working in each of the eight areas we'll discuss. That way you'll be able to see if you're on the correct course.

Compare this to a GPS navigation system in your car. It follows the same process of tracking. Not only does it need your destination; it also needs your starting point.

Then it plots the path you need to take in a series of small, discrete steps. If you take a wrong turn somewhere, the GPS needs to know in order to re-route you accordingly.

Without this tracking feature, a single wrong turn would mean you never reach your destination.

Many of you may never have considered tracking before. And you may not want to spend a great deal of money on tracking solutions that you're unsure of how to even use. At a minimum I would recommend that you install Google Analytics on your site and use that. As a free solution, it will provide you with a lot of insight on how people are interacting with your website.

When you can track the performance of individual parts of your business, you'll get a clearer picture of what parts are working well, and what parts are not.

When the business as a whole is performing well, many people would just be happy with that. However, if you drill down deeper, you may find that there is one part that is having a negative effect. Improve that one part, and your business will perform even better.

## Consideration #2: You Are Not Your Market

As a business owner, it's important to remember that you are not your market. When you look at things in your business, you'll see them from a business owner's perspective, not a consumer's perspective.

Often, what you think is best is not actually what will work best. That is something I've seen time and time again. Even in my own business I'm guilty of making that mistake. Sometimes it's hard to leave your ego out of this, but you have to trust the data and not your gut.

A classic example is web designers who want to produce the most aesthetically pleasing website. That may not be the kind of website that actually converts best. So-called "ugly" websites can often out-convert "pretty" websites, particularly in direct response situations.

Again, this is another reason why it's important to test.

If you're in doubt, test. Even if you're sure, test it anyway.

Every market is different, and every customer is different. So even if you've seen tests from other markets, don't assume the same result will hold true for you. Take them as a guide, not gospel.

The good news though, is that when you're going for simple 1% increases, you don't typically need to be testing a lot of different things, or be testing for a long time, to find that 1% increase.

## How the Process Breaks Down

The rest of the book will be broken down into three parts. Section one focuses on improving areas in your business before the sale – People, Prospects, and Purchases.

That's everything that happens up to the point when someone becomes a paying customer. There's still a lot of leverage, even before someone takes out their credit card to buy something from you. You can increase the number of people coming to your site, improve how they sign up to your site, and increase the conversions so more people become customers.

Section two will focus on everything that matters after someone has made that initial purchase with you – Products, Pricing, and Persistence.

You'll be focusing on ways to maximize the revenue per customer that you get – both the immediate revenue per customer and the lifetime revenue per customer. It's a lot easier and cheaper to sell something else to a current customer than it is to acquire a brand new customer.

Section three is dedicated less to customer-focused methods of business and more to the internal aspects – Productivity and Profitability.

These elements can be the least tangible of all the profit multipliers. But that also makes them a lot easier to leverage than all the others, because they're not reliant on getting more customers and sales. This section opens up opportunities for significant gains.

With my proven methodology you'll learn how to do all of those things without spending any more money on acquiring customers up front.

But what if you don't have your own business yet? Or at least not one that you can consider successful?

Don't worry. Everyone has to start somewhere.

To give you some inspiration I've included some bonus reports and case studies that outline some proven business models that I've built for myself and my clients.

One of the campaigns generated six figures a month, with another promotion doing six figures in a week. Many of these campaigns run almost completely on autopilot once established. You can download these reports and case studies to use them as a fast-start guide for building your own profitable business for free here.

www.SevenFigureBlueprints.com/bonuses

Okay, ready?

Let's get started!

PART 1

# BEFORE THE SALE

## Chapter 1

# PEOPLE

This first section will cover multiple ways to get more people to view your offers. Yes, you could just spend more on advertising, but my goal here is to teach you how to effectively use the assets you currently have.

The reasons for that are two-fold: first, it's often easier to build on what you already have, instead of starting a whole new campaign from scratch; second, paid advertising is not only very, very expensive, but it's also always a risk. Different sources perform differently, different offers have different results, and there are a lot of variables to consider with any kind of paid advertising campaign.

At this point in the process, we're assuming that we may not have any tracking software set up yet. If we do, we may not have a huge amount of tracking data to work with. We covered how important it is to have a good understanding of where you are, not just where you want to be. If you throw a bunch of money into paid advertising right now, you might get a return on it. But you also might not.

Additionally, the problem with so many variables is that you won't know which parts are working. As John Wanamaker, one of the forefathers of marketing, said, "Half the money I spend on advertising is wasted; the trouble is I don't know which half." That is where tracking becomes important.

In many cases, I've found the 80/20 rule applies, particularly in advertising. So it may not even be the case that half of the advertising is wasted. It could be that 80% is only bringing in 20% of the revenue, and the top 20% of advertising is bringing in 80% of the revenue.

Even a profitable campaign could be made more profitable if you simply trim the 80% that's not as effective. Spend that on the top 20% of advertising sources instead.

The effects of the 80/20 rule can be seen in many different ways. For example, if you're running Google AdWords advertising, you may find that 20% of your keywords are bringing you 80% of the sales. Similarly, if you advertise in newspapers, you may find that 20% of the publications bring you 80% of the sales. To get this granular level of detail, you need to have the tracking in place.

But even with free traffic methods, you will find that some methods give you a better return on your time than others. Put your focus on the methods that give you the best return.

In chapter three, we'll be looking at changes you can make to various parts of your sales process, with the goal of testing different elements to increase conversions. Those tests will lead to greater profitability, but they do take time to yield a result that's statistically significant.

The more people you have going through your sales process, the less time those tests will take. Focus on unlocking more traffic from your existing business, and you'll be able to run those tests faster and get results sooner.

If you know you've unlocked an extra 10% of targeted visits from your current business, then any paid advertising will yield 10% more visits for the same price. So you effectively pay less for each visitor.

## Turn One Visitor Into More

One of the best ways to unlock more traffic from your existing business is to leverage your existing customers. They are your very best brand ambassadors.

When you're selling online, you're dealing with people who have probably never met you, probably never even seen you, but your business has to build up enough trust to get them to make a purchase.

Trust is a huge factor with online sales, and if someone has pulled out their credit card and given you money, that means they trust you.

Not only that, but as consumers the mere act of purchasing something releases chemicals in our brain that make us feel excited. You have to make use of this state, since it is the ideal time to engage them.

## Leveraging New Customers

Once a customer has made a purchase from you, at the very least you should be trying to enlist their help to spread the word about your business. Take Amazon, for example. Every time I place an order with them, there's an option right there to share what I've just purchased to my Facebook wall. It's easy too. It's already pre-populated, so I can just click a link that will share the product, the description, and the link where someone else can buy it.

Think that brings in some extra sales for Amazon? Of course it does. They wouldn't do it unless they knew it worked. This is a really great way of getting more exposure for very, very little effort on your part.

An entrepreneur I know runs a company that sells hair extensions made of human hair. Alex runs this site with his wife, and they've built a very successful business. They built a lot of it using social media, particularly YouTube.

When someone purchases a set of hair extensions, they're obviously really excited about how they will look. They try them out, put the extensions in, and they're encouraged to take a picture and share it with their friends on Facebook/Instagram using the hashtag for the company.

There's a very obvious benefit to that – it helps generate referring traffic back to their website, so that anytime someone is sharing a picture, hundreds of people can see it. All those people's friends are potential new visitors.

Alongside that, there is a secondary benefit: social proof. Potential customers see their friends using the product and being genuinely excited about it. They're not just some unrelatable super model who was paid to look happy. This kind of social proof is huge for not only driving more traffic to the website, but also converting more of those people into actual customers.

It should go without saying that your product/service has to get good results for the customer to want to share it.

People are quick to complain on social media. But far fewer happy customers post reviews compared to unhappy customers. To ensure you make the most of the opportunity of positive feedback, actively lead your customers and ask them to give you good reviews. If you've made them happy, they'll want to do that for you. The hair extension brand is very much built around Alex and his wife. They're real, genuine people, and they generate a huge amount of value with the free videos they create. All that value and goodwill goes a long way if they ask someone to do them a favor and share a link, or a picture, of their purchase.

## Incentivizing

If you find that just asking people to share something on social media isn't generating much traction, the next step is to incentivize them in some way. One of the easiest ways to do that is to offer them a discount or financial reward if they can get a friend to become a customer.

It could be as simple as offering a store gift card, or a discount off their next purchase. It could even be an Amazon gift card. A monetary incentive like that is a huge motivator.

There are a couple of options you can take with this route and various levels of generosity. One method is to reward a customer if they can refer a friend who becomes a new customer. Another, potentially more powerful method is to have a double reward scheme. You reward the original referrer but also give the new customer a special discount or coupon. In this case, you're giving two rewards, but the conversions are likely to be higher because there is a stronger reason why, and also a sense of exclusivity. It's a lot easier to encourage someone to share that link when they can say, "Hey, if you use this link, you'll get a discount, and I'll get a gift card out of it."

If you haven't noticed it already, there's a huge benefit to these types of incentivization models – there is absolutely no financial risk to the business owner.

With these reward schemes, you are only paying out after someone has generated a new customer for you. Compare that to paid media where you pay out before you even receive a single visitor, and you'll see there is no guarantee of people becoming a customer at all.

Even though there is no risk for business owners, there are still very few who use something like this. I've found a lot of business owners to be risk averse and hesitant to try anything new, in case it turns out to be a money pit.

A friend of mine, who's a consultant, told me about a client of his. The client was using paid advertising with one particular platform and was generating an incredible return – roughly $30 for every $1 spent on advertising. When my consultant friend started working with him, he developed a plan on a different advertising platform. He was confident he could generate an additional revenue stream with a return of roughly $10 for every $1 spent. This was an additional source of revenue that didn't impact the initial advertising revenue stream in any way. Still, his client felt it was too expensive because it was "only" a 10:1 return, when he was already getting a 30:1 return.

Another example was a client who sold $10,000 coaching packages but was afraid to spend $10 per click with paid media. He felt that was too much when the industry average was more like $1-$2 per click. In his mind, $10 per click was way too expensive.

The truth is, it was expensive because it was so highly targeted. He could get a single $10,000 customer for every 100 clicks – or $1,000 in ad costs. So looking at the big picture, spending $1,000 to make $10,000 is a no-brainer. But if you just look at the $10-per-click figure, it's easy to get scared and pull the advertising campaign because you think it's costing too much.

Don't be afraid to use incentives in your marketing just because you're not sure they'll work. While they may take some time to set up, there is no monetary risk, so I recommend you at least attempt to implement them.

## Structuring the Incentive

Even though you're only paying out once someone generates a new customer for you, you obviously want to make sure you're not paying out more than you can afford to.

If you have an existing business in place, then you should already have a pretty good idea of how much it's costing you to acquire a new customer, and also how much each customer is worth to you. Ideally, you should have not just the initial customer value, but also metrics such as the 30-day value, 90-day value, and lifetime value.

Most customers won't buy just one thing from you. So long as you're providing good value in your products/services, and provided you have other relevant products/services to sell them, many customers will purchase more from you.

Ultimately, the easiest way to structure your incentive is to make sure the reward you're offering will be less than your lifetime value of that customer. Everything left after the reward will be your profit.

In many cases, it may be difficult to establish a lifetime value of a customer, particularly if you have only really just started tracking. In this case, one of the best ways to look at your reward is to work out your initial customer acquisition cost and make your reward be no more than that.

If you know you're currently spending $50 to acquire a $100 customer, then you could easily pay that $50 to a referring friend who brings in a new customer.

In reality, you could probably offer a lot less than $50 and still have someone motivated enough to refer other people. But in this case, you're spending that money on the reward rather than on advertising, for the same result.

Many customers would be happy with a $25 gift card in this scenario, so if you're normally spending $50 to acquire a customer, you're cutting your costs in half.

At a more extreme level, if you know you have a higher lifetime-customer value, you can even offer the full product price as a reward. For example, offer someone a $100 gift card if they refer a $100 customer. You make your profit on the backend.

One thing to note here is that when we're referring to the customer value, you should also factor in any costs you have. If you're selling digital information products, your fulfillment costs per customer will be minimal – probably just a few cents for the hosting bandwidth. If you have a physical product, you should factor in those costs and establish your profit per customer.

If a $100 customer only puts $50 profit into your pocket, your maximum reward should not exceed $50. Even if you pay out the full $50, you've acquired a new customer for free, and you should be able to generate more profits from them in the long term.

If you want to set up an incentive program, there are services online that provide that kind of functionality. FriendBuy.com and ReferralCandy.com are both sites (at the time of writing) that will handle everything: the reward processing, giving people individual links to share, tracking the rewards, and delivering them to customers once they hit certain targets.

## The Ultimate Incentive Program

While a simple incentive program can be effective, the ultimate incentive program is an affiliate program. This is another type of reward program where you pay a specific commission for every sale a person generates for you.

Affiliate programs get your customers involved in promoting your site. As an added bonus, it can also be a public affiliate program so that anyone can join and promote your site for you, not just paid customers. Each affiliate gets their own specific link, and they can promote it however they like (within the terms you set). Any time a sale is made through their referral link, that referring affiliate will be credited with a commission.

Again, there is absolutely zero financial risk to the business owner with this method, as you only have to pay out once you make a sale. Your affiliates will be the ones spending money on advertising, putting in the work to drive traffic to your site, and bringing you more customers. An affiliate program is an incredibly efficient way to build your business without spending any out-of-pocket expenses, or spending any time and energy on marketing. The affiliates handle this themselves.

It's important to provide affiliates with (a) an offer that converts well and (b) all the tools they need to go out and promote. Staying with the idea of leveraging your existing customers, it's possible with some affiliate platforms to automatically add each new customer to your affiliate program. That way, once they make a purchase from you, they're provided with their own affiliate link to share, and it's pre-populated with everything they need.

Beyond your existing customers, there are many professional affiliates whose entire business is built around promoting other companies in return for a commission. Those affiliates can bring you traffic (and sales) on a long-term basis, which is ultimately a lot more powerful than having a customer share a link once after a purchase.

The easiest way to get started with an affiliate program is to add your offer to an existing affiliate network. While you can run your own "in-house" affiliate program, the downside is that you need to first recruit your own affiliates.

There are sites such as CJ.com, Clickbank.com, and ShareASale.com that are all affiliate networks with a database of their own existing affiliates. By listing your offer with them, you have instant access to their pool of affiliates. If you're just getting started with an affiliate program, this is the best way, as it will give you immediate exposure.

## Co-Opetition

Outside of existing affiliate networks, look at any existing relationships you have in the marketplace. It doesn't always have to be other affiliate marketers. You could even work with other product owners in your space. I like to use the term "co-opetition" – competition you co-operate with.

Find people with products or services that are similar or complementary to your own, without competing directly. Then work together to promote each others products, e.g. in your email sequence or within your thank you pages.

As an example, let's assume you sell a course on "how to make money in real estate".

If you found someone else who sold a course on "how to make money in stocks", they could potentially be a great person to cooperate with.

They're two different products, but they could be complementary to the same audience. Someone interested in real estate could also be interested in stocks.

By cross-promoting products, you open yourself up to a whole new set of customers you may otherwise not have had access to.

One question I often get about this approach is, "Why would I want to send my customers to someone else?" The obvious answer is that they will send their customers to you in return.

But more importantly, you aren't the only person your customer is spending money with. They have probably signed up to multiple mailing lists, getting offers from multiple businesses on a daily basis.

The truth is, we're all consumers by nature. When we're interested in a certain topic, we try to absorb all the information we can on that topic, often buying lots of different related products. At least by partnering with other people, you have the opportunity to have them send you customers too.

As an added bonus, when you cross-promote with others in your market, it gives you an additional income stream. For any sales you make for the other person, you should be getting a commission. If you can send someone 100 buyers for their $2,000 course, you could earn $100,000 at a 50% commission rate.

In one of my own info-product businesses, I have a follow-up sequence of my own products promoted to customers. Once they reach the end of that sequence, I'll promote other related offers as an affiliate. Any sales from those affiliate offers are additional revenue that I would otherwise have missed out on.

## Structuring Your Affiliate Program

When it comes to structuring your affiliate program, follow the same line of thinking as the customer incentive program. Figure out how much profit you make per customer and pay less than that in affiliate commission.

However, it's important to realize that many affiliates are serious business owners themselves with the potential to send you traffic on a long-term basis. Make sure you're doing everything you can to make that happen.

Most businesses sell more than one product to customers. If you're in a market like the information marketing space, it's likely you'll have a range of price points, with many higher-priced products in your sales funnel.

Instead of just paying affiliates based on the frontend sale, consider paying them based on the total revenue that could be generated by a customer experiencing the whole sales funnel.

You could either structure this in such a way that affiliates get a cut on everything their customer purchases, or you could structure it in such a way that they get a higher affiliate commission up front.

One partner of mine used to pay out 200% commissions to his affiliates. That meant for every $20 product one of his affiliates sold, they would receive a $40 commission. As you can imagine, it got a lot of people promoting that particular offer. He was able to do it because he had a well-structured backend funnel with different products at multiple price points, and even a coaching package. Each $20 customer was worth considerably more over the next 30 days than the $40 he paid out in commissions.

Here's an example of how it might look for him:

Affiliate sends 100 sales for $2,000 in revenue, and seller pays out $4,000 in commissions. Seller has a loss of $2,000 at this point.

Ten percent of initial buyers purchase a $100 upgrade product for another $1,000 in revenue. Seller has a loss of $1,000 at this point.

1% of initial buyers join a $5,000 coaching program. Seller has a profit of $4,000 at this point.

Paying out 200% doesn't look as crazy now, right?

Another marketer I know paid 300% commission on the frontend sales. Again,

he knew he could do this because he was tracking everything.

He knew that for every 100 new customers, one would join his coaching program.

One hundred new customers would be worth $6,000 in total revenue - $1,000 in initial sales + $5,000 in coaching sales.

He paid out 300% commissions on the $10 frontend, which was $30. A loss of $20 on each frontend sale.

But each new customer was worth an average of $60 within 30 days.

So even though he paid 300% on that first sale, it only amounted to 50% of the total value of that customer in the first 30 days. He kept the other 50%, which all came from customers other people had sent him – he did nothing to generate that revenue.

It's easy to look at this and wonder how you can implement it in your own business, and if it's even possible to pay out those amounts. The truth is, you probably never will need to go to these lengths. These examples are to show you that once you have a good handle on your numbers, you can structure your affiliate program to make it as attractive as possible for people to promote. The more affiliates you have, the more traffic you can get. The happier those affiliates are, the longer they'll keep promoting.

Work out the initial customer value you have. Then the 30-day, 60-day, and 90-day revenue numbers. Those are some good benchmarks to establish.

If you only have one product, then they will all be the same, because you're not making any more revenue off of each customer. Ideally, you'll have more than one product. Then you track how many more of those products customers purchase from you. From that, work out what each customer is worth to you in an average of 90 days.

Lifetime customer value is a good metric to know, but for the sake of setting up an affiliate program, it's not always that helpful. A high lifetime value is great. But not if it takes you 10 years on average to get that. You can't pay out 300% commissions, and then wait 10 years to make a profit.

In my own business, I look at the immediate revenue per customer, and I'm happy to give up to 100% of that to affiliates. I know I'll be able to generate more over time. The worst-case scenario in this situation is that I've got a new buyer and it cost me nothing to acquire.

You may not need to give that much in your own business. You may find there are plenty of affiliates who are happy with a smaller percentage.

One thing to consider is your click-to-sales conversion ratio. The higher you can make your conversion rate, the lower you can make the affiliate payout while still keeping it attractive. Many affiliates will look at a product on an EPC (Earnings Per Click) basis. A product with a high conversion but lower payout can give a better EPC compared to a product with a higher payout but significantly lower conversions. Ultimately, affiliates just want to know what will make them the most revenue per visitor that they send.

## How to Set Up Long-Term Affiliate Promotions

Earlier, we talked about using co-opetition for finding opportunities to cross-promote with other business owners. One of the best ways of doing this for long-term traffic and sales is integration marketing. Instead of focusing on a one-time promotion, your goal is to establish a long-term promotion. Once set up, long-term promotion will continue to send you a steady stream of new customers.

Imagine for a second that someone purchases a product and they are directed to a post-purchase page. For digital products, this could be a simple download page or a member's welcome page. For a physical product, this could even be a welcome letter they receive in the actual package. This is the ideal place to have someone integrate your product.

Let's reconsider the previous example of the 'co-opetition' products. You have a product on "how to make money with stocks". A competitor has a product on "how to make money with real estate".

You could approach the owner of that real estate product and provide them with a bonus they give to their customers. It could be a free report on how to get started making money with stocks. That free report leads into the fully paid product on how to make money with stocks.

Positioned like this, it can be a bonus that adds value to their original offer, and it also gives you a way to collect the name and email of these brand new buyers at no cost. For any sales that result from that integration, you pay the other person a 50% commission and keep the other 50% for yourself.

Setting up this kind of deal gives you a constant stream of new buyers being exposed to your offers. Don't get me wrong, one-time promotions are still great if you can get nothing else, but integration marketing is a much more sustainable, long-term solution.

One of my own businesses was built almost entirely through integration marketing. I would focus on people who had similar complementary products but who didn't have a sales funnel that was as developed as it could be. My offer gave them the chance to get more revenue from each customer they got. They were happy to send the traffic to me, so it was a win-win situation.

In this case, the product was sold via an automated webinar. All the partner had to do was include a link on their thank you page with a short blurb on how/why someone should attend it. To make it even easier, I gave them the blurb so they just had to copy and paste it.

The key to making this work is to nurture those relationships and make sure your affiliates are happy. Going back to the 80/20 rule, I found that in this particular business of mine it was more like a 90/10 rule. It worked out that 10% of my affiliates were bringing in 90% of the revenue.

People are inherently lazy, so make it as easy as possible for them to promote. Give them everything they need. If they need an email to send out to their customer database, then write that email for them, so all they have to do is copy and paste, and hit send.

If you want them to integrate the offer into their thank you page, make sure you create the graphics/copy for them, so all they need to do is copy and paste it onto their page. Your goal is to make it so easy that it's impossible for them to find a reason not to follow through.

This also means they're less likely to go and look for something else to promote. If you're giving them the tools they need and if you're paying them well and on time, it will be too much work for them to go out and research new offers.

Going back to an example of my own business, one of my best affiliates was someone who created new products every two or three months. He probably could have researched different offers to promote on the backend of that, but ultimately, he knew he was getting paid well with mine, that I always paid him on time, and that his customers were taken care of. As a result, he was happy to keep my offer integrated and keep sending me buyers from every new product he created.

An important point to remember is that not all affiliate relationships will last forever so it's crucial to be constantly recruiting new affiliates. When you have 10% of affiliates bringing in 90% of the revenue, it can be devastating if just one stops promoting for you. The bigger the pool of affiliates you have, the more stable your business will be.

## Other Ways to Leverage Existing Traffic

Remember, we're only looking for a 10% increase at each point here, so you don't need to use all these methods at the beginning. My goal, however, is to make sure you have options to scale up as and when you want to. Just because we're only aiming for a 10% increase in each area, that doesn't mean we won't welcome 20% or 30% increases.

## Viral Marketing

Depending on the business you have, viral marketing can be an effective strategy for increasing traffic. Not every business lends itself well to this type of marketing, and typically, the share-worthy content is not based around trying to sell a specific product but more around building brand awareness. If you have shareable content, then the most important thing is to make sure it's easy to share. Shared traffic doesn't cost you anything, so every single share you get has the potential for more traffic.

Quizzes can be a particular type of viral content that works well too, especially on social media. It's easy to share content on Facebook.

You've probably seen a lot of them, such as "What type of person are you?" or "What character from this TV show are you?" People like to take these types of quizzes and will often share the results with others.

You can use these quizzes to ask people for their email address so you can send them their results. That will help you build a list of prospects, which we'll cover in the next chapter.

Controversy is always good for shareable content. Controversial topics work well because they polarize people. When people are polarized in one way, they are more passionate. They may love it or hate it, but so long as they are passionate about the topic, they will be engaged. Think about presidential elections and the mass of content that gets shared online. If you look at the most shared content, it's the posts that have some more extreme claim or element.

Contests are another tool you can use to get people sharing your content. Several different services were built for this specific purpose. One of my favorite tools is UpViral.com, which allows you to run contests and incentivized promotions, and which handles all the tracking/rewards.

In a contest, you can offer a single prize, or even prizes to everyone who reaches a certain target. That target could be something as simple as sharing a link on Facebook and Twitter, or it could be more complex, such as getting three people to buy a product from your link. The easier it is to claim the reward, the more likely people are to share it.

## Leveraging Existing Content

If you're selling anything online, then you probably have some form of content somewhere. It could be a blog with content, YouTube videos, or press releases you've submitted.

One of the easiest ways to get more traffic is to leverage those content pieces you already have and repurpose them in multiple different ways.

A blog post can easily be repurposed into a PowerPoint presentation and submitted to slide directories such as SlideShare.net. Record your screen while narrating the PowerPoint, and that becomes an instant video you can upload to YouTube and other video directories. Take the audio from that video to create a mini-podcast. Take a selection of blog posts and rework them into a book or an e-book to upload on Kindle.

All of these become unique content pieces on their own. The work required to repurpose one piece of content into five different types of content is a lot less than trying to create five unique pieces of content. Submitting each of these repurposed pieces to the relevant directories can help bring in more traffic to your site.

Finally, if you get any traffic from the search engines, it is really worth taking the time to do a full traffic analysis. Find out what pages on your site are getting you traffic, and what keywords are bringing visitors to your sites from the search engines.

It's incredibly easy to spot opportunities based on what's already working well with your site. If a page on your site is ranking on the second page of the search results, promote that page more. You'll get better results compared to creating a new page.

If you have pages and keywords that are performing well, continue to build backlinks to them. That will help your site rise even further. The closer you are to the top of the first page of results, the more traffic you can get.

The great thing about search engine traffic is that, while it is not technically free (since you have to invest time in promotion, and possibly money in the content creation), once a site is ranking well, it can continue to bring in passive traffic even after the promotion has stopped. A full tutorial on search engine optimization is beyond the scope of this book, but the simple tips above will help you take what you already have and give you some ideas on ways to reach your goal of a 10% increase.

Chapter 2

# PROSPECTS

Now that you've been generating more traffic to your site, the next step is to convert those cold visitors into warm prospects. A cold visitor has no idea who you are, or what you have to offer. They're completely new to your business. A warm prospect is someone who's not yet a customer but who is more qualified than a cold visitor.

One way to view this is to imagine a real-world situation. If you have a retail store, hundreds of people walk by your store every day. Most will not ever set foot inside the premises, let alone make a purchase from you. In the online world, those people typically comprise 90% or more of all your visitors.

Prospects are people who may decide to step inside your shop and have a look around. They're not necessarily someone who rushes to the front desk knowing exactly what they want to buy. But once they step inside the shop, they're interested enough to take a closer look at what you have to offer. In turn, you have the opportunity to take time to communicate with them directly. You can find out what they're looking for and what their needs are. With that information, you help them find a solution to their problem or direct them to a product that fits their needs.

A prospect in this state is much more likely to turn into a customer making a purchase at some point in the future. Even if they don't buy immediately, you've made a connection with them. That connection means they are more likely to purchase from you over someone they've had no interaction with.

Online, a prospect is typically someone who has entered their name and email, or some other personal identifiable information, on your website. This allows you to continue a conversation with them rather than them leaving your website, never to return.

To communicate with your prospects, you'll want to invest in a tool called an autoresponder. You can use it to create a database of leads and email them all from one dashboard. I'll cover autoresponders and the best ways to use them further on in this chapter, but for now, let's focus on getting those prospects.

## Go for the Lead or the Sale?

Should you be going for the lead and nurturing that prospect, or instead going directly for the sale? In a lot of markets, particularly online, average sales conversion rates from cold traffic are between one and three percent. That means out of every 100 visitors, 97-99 of them may leave and never come back. If you're putting the time, effort, and money into generating those visitors, it's a waste to let 99% of them go without ever getting anything from them.

Don't get me wrong, it's definitely possible to run a profitable business with a 1% conversion rate from visitors to sales. But the goal here is to determine if it is the *most* profitable way to run your business.

If you focus purely on lead generation, it's possible to get 25-50% or more of all the visitors you're generating to give you their name and/or email to become a lead. To keep the numbers simple, let's assume you're getting 50% of people to become a lead. Then assume you get just 2% of all those leads to turn into customers at some point after following up with them. Do that, and you're making the same revenue as getting just 1% of all cold visitors to buy immediately from the sales page on their only visit.

The benefit with the lead generation campaign is that you can follow up with leads who didn't initially purchase. You should be able to convert more of these leads over time through regular follow-ups. You can also generate additional revenue through sending them other offers – either your own, or offers as an affiliate.

The downside is there will be a group of people who won't enter their name and email, so they'll never see your sales page. In that group, there may be people who would have purchased from you if they'd gone straight to the sales page.

This is something you should test because each market is different. Even if you go for the direct sale approach, you are still building a list – it is just a much smaller list consisting only of buyers. You can promote more products to this buyer list and increase revenue that way.

There is no hard or fast rule that says which method is best. The best method for your business may be a combination of these two models. If you already have an existing business that is profitable by just going for the sale, the hybrid method below is the ideal place to start testing without upsetting your current sales process.

## The Hybrid Method

When people visit your webpage, the majority will leave either by hitting the back button on their browser or by closing the browser window entirely. There are simple tools that detect when this is about to happen and display a custom message. Those are called 'exit-intent' messages, since they are triggered by the web browser detecting the user's intention to leave.

At that point, you can use a message to get a visitor's name and email address in exchange for something of value to them. That could be a free report, a free trial/chapter/sneak-peek of your product, or a coupon in exchange for their information. The key is to make it a valuable offer that is relevant to the product they were just considering.

It's possible to get 10% or more people to enter their name and email using one of these types of exit-intent messages. Once they do, it gives you the ability to follow up with them and continue the conversation, with the goal of converting them at some point in the future.

Remember, throughout this process, we're not looking to double our sales in one fell swoop. Tiny gains at each point can yield large improvements overall. If you can get 10% of all people to enter their name and email, you will be able to convert some of those into sales. Each additional sale will have a positive effect on your bottom line.

Once you have this list, you can market to them over and over. Even if they don't purchase the original offer they saw, there's no reason they won't buy something else. As long as you follow up with them and present them with other offers, they may buy more from you as well.

## Getting Into Your Customer's Mind

When determining whether to go for the lead or the sale, you don't have to use the same approach throughout the whole of your business. You'll typically have traffic coming from multiple sources, and each visitor may be in a different place in terms of how much they need your product/service.

There will be the crowd that has the 'bleeding neck', i.e. people with an extremely urgent issue. You should provide them with the solution up front. Don't try to turn them into a lead and nurture a sale over a period of days.

For example, anyone searching for a plumber or locksmith is an example of a 'bleeding neck' prospect. You typically don't search for a plumber unless you have an urgent need for one. It would make no sense for a plumber to have a squeeze page with a free report, and then 14 days of content, before going for a sale. Similarly, someone looking for a locksmith probably needs urgent assistance. A free report on how to avoid getting locked out of your house is redundant in that situation.

When developing your lead generation plan, consider where your prospects are coming from and where in the sales cycle they are likely to be. If they're a 'bleeding neck' prospect, go directly for the sale. If they're just browsing for information and have no urgent need, get their name/email. Then follow up with them and build that relationship with them. They may not have an urgent need at that moment, but you'll have a greater chance of being the person they buy from when their need changes.

## Get More Sales From Your Prospects

Whether you build a list or not, there will always be 1-3% of visitors who buy immediately from your sales page. At the other end of the spectrum, there are probably ~50% of people who have no actual need for your product at that time. It's the remaining visitors you want to focus on with your prospect campaign – those that are interested but not urgently enough to buy right away.

There are a few reasons why interested prospects may not buy from you immediately. Trust is one of the main reasons. Many times, people just don't believe you can help them. Even if they like what you have to offer, they may have some niggling doubts in their mind. They'll go away to do a quick Google and research your company, or to compare your services with someone else's.

If you can communicate with them, you are able to build up that trust over time. As the trust is built up, you increase your chances of them becoming a customer. An easy way to do that is to let people see you as a real person in your communications. People like to buy from those they like, know, and trust. When you email, write in a way that is relatable and doesn't make you look like a faceless corporation. You can use email follow-ups to send case studies and testimonials of other customers. Show that your product works for people just like them. All of this builds that trust.

Timing also plays its part. Everyone is busy these days, and it's essential that you're able to effectively follow up with your prospects. As mobile devices become more prevalent, a large percentage of people are browsing the internet on a device that is constantly pulling them in different directions. Text messages, Facebook notifications, and Twitter notifications are all distractions.

It's easy for someone to be looking at your site one minute, and then doing three or four other things over the course of the next minute. They could be incredibly interested in what you have to offer, but the distractions mean they don't get a chance to make a purchase. If you have their email address, you can follow up with them and bring them back to your site over and over. They may get temporarily distracted, but they don't have to be lost forever.

The truth is that most sales come from follow-ups. Studies have shown that out of all people who may purchase a product, 80% will need at least five exposures to your offer.

Think about that. If you're not doing at least five follow-ups in your marketing, you're likely only getting 20% of the potential sales you could be getting. With an online business, the easiest way to achieve those multiple exposures is an email list. You can get some additional exposure through methods such as ad retargeting, but there you're restricted to displaying banners on sites. With email, you have the ability to communicate a lot more and build that relationship effectively.

Another benefit of this constant communication is that you have the 'top-of-the-mind awareness' of your prospects. Even if you're doing at least five follow-ups, as many as 60% of all people who go on to become a customer won't purchase for at least three months. Of all people who eventually become customers, 20% won't purchase within 12 months.

In an ideal world, that means your follow-up sequence should extend to at least 12 months to convert as many prospects as possible. In practice, however, that may not be the easiest thing to do, given the considerable amount of time, effort, and money it will take.

You can be constantly building your follow-up sequence as you send out new emails, though. Start by writing the emails for your first 30-day follow-up sequence. That will give you the best chance of converting at least a good portion of your new prospects into additional sales. As you send out more emails to your prospects, take each new email and add it to your follow-up sequence in your autoresponder. Your follow-up sequence will grow organically from this.

I've seen lots of cases in my own business of prospects being on my list for months, or even years, before they make a purchase. But there's a really good example of someone who was able to convert *me* into a customer after I'd been a non-paying prospect for a long time.

Ben Settle is an email marketing genius and hugely successful marketer. You might go as far as calling him an anti-marketer. His whole business is built on the premise that he likes to work as little as possible, and he actively discourages certain people from becoming his customers. He's also a great example of showing prospects that he is a real person and not a faceless corporation.

Ben runs the paid newsletter at EmailPlayers.com. His subscribers get a printed monthly newsletter on how to make more money with their email list. He also gives away a free PDF version of one newsletter on his site for anyone that enters their name and email.

Way back, I had subscribed as a non-paying prospect to receive the PDF, and over the next six months, I was receiving a daily email from Ben. I mentioned he's not your typical marketer, and he sends out a very specific style of email – daily. The reason he can get away with it is that not every single email contains a hard pitch. He uses a combination of information and entertainment – or what he calls 'infotainment'.

While his emails always have an offer of some sorts, they also have an inherent value because they're entertaining. The pitches he makes are always tied into the story or lesson he's sharing. It may only be a subtle tie-in so you don't feel like you're being sold to.

I found myself on his list for six months or more, reading those emails. Finally, I joined his paid newsletter, simply because of the content in his daily emails. I've been a customer ever since. This is one of the only subscriptions I have in my business of which I'm actively happy to see the payment go out each month. Ben's emails do a great job of selling prospects on becoming customers, but they do an even better job of re-selling existing customers on the benefits of remaining a customer.

If you have a moment, I would recommend checking out his site. But the real point of this story was that it took me six months of getting emails from Ben before I became a customer. I'm pretty sure there are many, many more of his current customers that have joined as a result of one of the follow-up emails. Without those follow-ups, he simply wouldn't have as many customers as he does now.

## How Often Should You Email Your List?

This is what we call a 'frequently asked question'. The real answer is that there's no exact number of emails you should be sending to your list. What I have found, though, is that the more I email, the more sales I make.

It's important that the emails have value to the customer in some way. That value may be that they're getting a coupon or discount. The value could just be that the email is entertaining. If you're constantly sending people hard-pitch emails, you're likely to see low response rates and people unsubscribing.

As mentioned above, Ben Settle sends an email to his subscribers every single day. When he's running a special promotion, he'll send more than one email a day. Another marketer I know sends four emails a day to his list. He follows the same kind of infotainment model as Ben, and he's confirmed that the more he emails, the more sales he makes.

Four emails a day is definitely on the extreme end of the spectrum, but there are also lots of people who are scared to email too much and who only send an email once a month. In my opinion, that's worse than emailing four times a day. Why? Because you're missing out on a huge amount of revenue.

When you're scared of emailing because you're afraid people will complain or unsubscribe, you're costing your business money. Not only are you missing out on revenue, but people who complain are not your ideal customers anyway.

If you're using an autoresponder service, you are charged for each person on your list. It may only be a small amount, but if they won't turn into a customer, it's better to have them unsubscribe sooner rather than later. If they will never buy from you, there is no point in them being on your list and costing you money.

Another factor to consider is that most people these days get upwards of 100 emails a day. Of those, they'll maybe open 20 and click on links in two or three of them.

If you're only emailing once a month, you could be competing with 3,000 other emails in their inbox. The most common scenario is that your message will just get lost in the crowd. If people do happen to see your message, they may have forgotten who you are and why you're emailing them.

When you send emails more frequently, you're increasing the chances of your messages being seen. You're increasing your prospect's awareness of you, and also the likelihood they will purchase from you. It's simple maths, but the more offers you can put in front of people's eyeballs, the more sales you will make.

## Putting the Pieces Together

Earlier in the chapter, we talked about using an autoresponder to handle the bulk of the work in managing an email list. With that process, we are looking for gains – both in terms of revenue and in terms of efficiency. There's little point in building an email list if you have to send out hundreds of emails personally every single day.

Thankfully, there are services that make sending an email to a list of 10,000 people as easy as sending an email to just one person. With an autoresponder service (such as GetResponse.com or AWeber.com), every prospect's details will be stored in a database. It will contain their name, email, and any other information they submitted. It will also contain important information, such as their IP address and time stamps of registration, which are important for staying compliant with spam laws.

Once prospects join your list, they can receive a set of pre-written emails with a pre-determined time frame. That means every lead will receive the same sequence of emails, regardless of when they sign up. All of these are sent automatically, which is useful for generating passive sales from every lead that enters their information on your site.

In addition to the follow-up emails, you can also send out broadcast emails. Those are emails you send to your entire list (or a specific group) all at the same time. That type of marketing is perfect for limited-time special offers with a real deadline, for example during certain holidays.

An autoresponder that's set up correctly is an incredibly powerful tool. It will allow you to send those important follow-up messages with minimal effort. The great thing is that you do the work once and get the rewards long into the future.

Focus on creating one email a day, and add that email to the end of your follow-up sequence so that every future lead will also see it. Do that for a year. You'll have a huge series of emails that will automatically go out to every single lead. That will have a massive impact on the conversions you get over time.

The benefits of autoresponders are not just limited to their ease of handling all the emails. Once you have a database of subscribers, it will also provide you with a lot of data and insight into how they react.

You'll be able to look at the stats and see what types of emails get the best results. You'll have the ability to split test emails by sending one email to half your list, another email to the other half, and directly comparing the response to those two emails. You then take the winning version and add that to your follow-up sequence. With the power the autoresponder gives you, it's very easy to make that 10% improvement just by testing your follow-up sequences.

For example, if you have a list of 20,000 subscribers, you send one version of an email to 10,000, and a second version to the other 10,000. If one version generates 100 sales and the other generates 125 sales, you know the second version has performed 25% better. Now use that second email over and over again by putting it in your follow-up sequence, and you've given yourself a

25% bump on the revenue you generate from all future leads.

## What to Test in Your Emails

When it comes to split testing emails, the most obvious thing to test is the subject line. If the subject line doesn't compel the person to open the email, they'll never click the link and buy. Do not underestimate the power of split testing headlines. Don't restrict yourself to just testing two subject lines. Test three, four, five, or more variations and see which one performs better.

One thing to keep in mind with split testing like this is that, ultimately, making a sale should be the goal. While one subject line may get a much higher open rate, if the email overall converts sales at a lower rate, then don't use it.

Next test the email body length itself. Shorter emails often get more clicks because it's easy to scan through the email, find the link, and click it. However, that doesn't always convert into more sales.

A longer email may do more pre-selling, which can disqualify people. As a result, you may end up with a much lower click-through rate, but those people clicking through are more qualified. That can give a better conversion rate to sales overall. Again, this is why it's important to track and look at the campaign as a whole and not just the individual elements.

One tip when running a promotion over a period of a few days is that, towards the end of the promotion, it works better to send shorter emails at a higher frequency.

In my own business, my email on the first day of the promotion could be a relatively longer email of 300-400 words. The goal is to outline the offer and the main benefits to the prospects. However, on the last day of the promotion, the goal of the email is simply to remind them the offer will be closing soon.

At this point, they're probably familiar with the promotion, so they don't need a big long email again. You just want them to take action and order.

Typically, I'll send one email a couple of hours before the promotion ends. It's really short, saying something like, "Hey, this page is coming down in two hours – have you seen it yet? Here's the link." That's it. Again, people may be distracted or may have forgotten about the offer, so you're just bringing it back to their attention. When you couple that with the scarcity of an impending deadline, it helps to get a lot of people purchasing.

Considering how many people view emails on a mobile device, it's important your emails are easy to read. That means you'll want to keep the line lengths short, use short paragraphs, and consider using slightly larger text. If people have to do a lot of sideways scrolling, squinting, or zooming just to be able to read your message, they'll be a lot less likely to click on the links within it.

## What to Offer to Get the Lead

You've got your first follow-up sequence planned out and a few emails in place in your autoresponder. Now it's time to focus on getting more of those leads. To do that, you'll need to have something to offer them so that they'll share their email address with you.

When someone gives you their name and email, they should be getting some value in exchange. That exchange of value should help establish your credibility and authority, as well as help the prospect solve a problem.

The best results can come from something that gives your prospect a 'quick win'. It could be a small report or something that gives them a piece of bite-sized information they can immediately apply and get a result with. That is really good for establishing trust.

Examples include:

- Free reports with a set of proven steps they can follow.
- A simple software application that helps them to do something faster/easier.
- A short video training showing something that will help them solve their problem.

It really depends on your product or service. Think of what you can give/show someone that will provide them with value, as well as move them closer to becoming your customer.

Your free offer does need to have some kind of value to the prospect. By that I don't just mean monetary value, but a tangible value they'll get from the exchange. You could tell people they'll get a free report that normally sells for $27, but that may have no real value to them. On the other hand, if you tell them the report can help them lose a minimum of 10 pounds in the next 30 days, then they can put a value on that for themselves.

Personally, I've had a lot of success by offering webinars to potential prospects. A person can sign up for a webinar just by entering their name and email on a registration page. Then, in a group setting, I can demonstrate or teach a particular skill for 45-60 minutes and present an offer after that.

For the best results, the content should be high quality and give them information they can apply after the webinar, whether they buy from you or not. Webinars are a powerful tool, as you are able to interact with the viewers. That interaction goes a long way in building rapport and trust. More importantly, prospects can ask you direct questions and get specific answers from you.

If you're just starting out, you may be intimidated by the thought of organizing webinars. You may have seen people hosting large events with 1,000 or more people on them. In reality, you can hold small webinars using something like Zoom, with just a handful of people. They are great for gaining insight into your customers. The conversations you have can help you come up with ideas for content to send in your emails too.

Many online businesses have a blog, or a place where they post content online. Those make ideal places to try and convert more visitors into prospects. A method that works well is creating what's called a 'content upgrade'. Essentially, this is a piece of content that builds on the information provided in the original blog post.

For example, if you had a blog post that talks about how to get more website traffic, your content upgrade could be a PDF with 25 different traffic methods they can download and print out. Alternatively, it could be an action plan or worksheet. It could even be just a PDF of the actual blog post so that they can keep it on their computer to refer back to. But it's something directly related to the content they've just read. Those types of opt-in bribes convert at a much better rate than a more general, unrelated offer.

## Advanced Strategies

When building your list, consider creating a hot list in your sales process. This is something I don't see a huge amount of people do, but it lets you target the mostly qualified prospects and focus your efforts on them.

When someone goes to the checkout page on your site, they're presented with a whole bunch of fields they need to fill in. Not everyone who reaches this page will turn into a customer. In fact, cart abandonment is a huge issue in itself (but that will also give us opportunities later to claw back some of those lost sales).

A good way to combat this is to first have people enter their name and email when they click the order button. After that, they are redirected to the full checkout page. That strategy ensures you can follow up with those hot prospects. If they've read your sales page, clicked the order button, and filled out their name and email but haven't yet ordered, then chances are it won't take much to get them off the fence.

You'll have a separate follow-up sequence for those leads that focuses on helping them complete their order. Create an email that goes out 30-60 minutes after they enter their info and only gets sent out to them if they didn't complete a purchase. The email can simply ask them if they need any help or remind them to check out while directing back to that page.

If they don't buy, send them more emails which are more conversion focused, e.g. FAQ emails, customer testimonials, discounts, even personal help. You may not be able to recover all of those sales, but again, every little gain can compound over time.

It should be mentioned here that most autoresponder services provide the ability to segment your leads based on their activity. In the example above, the person starts on the prospect list. When they go to check out, they sign up to a new list (the hot list).

The segmentation technology in the autoresponder removes them from the prospect list so that they don't keep getting regular prospect emails. Similarly, once they make a purchase, they get automatically added to a buyer list and removed from the hot list.

Segmentation is extremely powerful when done correctly, and it's not just limited to the scenario above. If you have a range of products, each of those should be on a specific list within your autoresponder. Similarly for each different lead magnet you have. This way you're separating people based on their interests, and you can send them the most relevant offers. The more specific and targeted your sales messages, the better your results will be.

You'll also find that your buyer leads are likely to be a lot more responsive than your non-paying leads. You can send higher-priced products to buyer leads and move them through a sequence that's designed to provide them with more value at higher prices. That is all part of the relationship-building process.

You wouldn't necessarily try and sell a new subscriber on a $10,000 coaching package. However, if you have a subscriber who's gone from being a non-paying prospect, to a $100 customer, to a $500 customer, to a $2,000 customer, they will be much more receptive to the $10,000 package.

It's just like dating. You don't go out and ask for someone's hand in marriage immediately after meeting them. That usually doesn't work. You go for a smaller commitment first, such as grabbing a coffee. There's a natural progression to the relationship.

It's the same thing with email marketing. You need to start off small, introduce yourself, let them know who you are, and build on that. If they feel you're a good fit for them, they'll move from prospect to customer. (The exception to this would be those 'bleeding neck' customers who don't need convincing; they just need to know where to make a purchase.)

The segmentation technology means you'll be able to manage that relationship with tens of thousands of different people automatically. When you're focusing on the customer's needs and providing them with the right offers, at the right time, that's when you're able to maximize the revenue from each prospect.

Finally, surveys are another way to take advantage of segmentation. If you have a general list of prospects, send them to a survey and have them be automatically segmented based on which options they choose. Then they can get emails that are much more tailored to their specific needs. In many cases, you can sell the same product to each segment and get higher conversions by segmenting. Simply change the message each prospect receives based on the segment they're in so that you're speaking to them in a more targeted way.

An example for the weight loss market would be to ask them why they want to lose weight. Is it to fit in their old clothes? Is it to have more energy? Is it to impress someone particular? The outward results of losing weight are the same, but the internal desire can be different for each person. Uncover that desire and feed it back into your marketing. That way, your marketing messages will resonate more with them.

## A Warning – My Mistake

There's something I must stress at this point. A mailing list is one of the biggest assets you'll ever create in your business. Don't underestimate its potential. As such, you should treat it like any other asset in your business and invest in a professional service.

Many years ago, when I was first getting started in digital marketing, I was a student in university, which meant I had very little disposable income. In other words, I was cheap as hell. I built my first list of prospects using a free autoresponder service that enabled me to grow a list of around 1,000 subscribers.

Everything was going great: I was making sales and constantly adding new leads to my database. Then one day, the guy running the service decided he had enough of maintaining a free service and just shut it down.

Overnight, my list was gone. With it went my business at that point and any future revenue from that list. That was a huge wake-up call. The next thing I did was invest $15 in a GetResponse.com account. I've been with them ever since and alongside my domains/hosting accounts, it's the most important part of my business.

That's a warning for everyone reading this. If you're building a list or growing your existing list, don't skimp on the cost. A professional service is not that expensive.

Although my goal with this book is to help you use the existing assets you have without spending more, this is one of the cases where a minimal investment is recommended. This investment has the potential to bring huge gains on its own.

Chapter 3

# PURCHASES

Getting more traffic to your site and building a large list of subscribers is useless if nobody goes on to buy anything from you. As an entrepreneur, you're in business to make money. To do that, you need people to get out their credit cards. In this section, I'll show you methods to turn more visitors and prospects into customers.

If you have an existing business, you'll already be getting customers from your current sales process. But there are always different ways to get higher conversion rates with your current traffic. As I've been saying throughout the book, you're not looking to massively increase conversions. You don't need to go from a 1% conversion to a 10% conversion. You just want a *relative* increase of 10%. That means going from 1% to 1.1%. Remember that your goal is only to find those marginal gains, and it's easy to create a plan of action and implement it quickly.

There is a significant number of elements in the sales process that you'll be able to work with. To cover them all would not only take up too much time but likely overwhelm you too. Therefore, in this chapter, I'll show you some of the techniques that are most likely to get you a positive increase in a short amount of time.

With an online business, you will be selling via a website rather than face to face. That type of sales can be quite impersonal. However, it gives lots of scope for testing. Through testing, you'll discover what works better across all customers.

Most websites fall into one of two main categories. The first is a direct-response-style website. Those sell with long sales copy, a video sales letter, or perhaps a combination of both. The other main type of site is an e-commerce site. Here you may have multiple products for sale, but even this type of site will still have sales copy and possibly also videos, images, and other elements that contribute to the overall sales process. Both of these sites have multiple areas you can run tests on.

When starting out with testing, the simplest method is to run a straight A/B split test. In this type of test, you have two almost identical pages. You'll pick one element you want to test, e.g. a headline. The headline will be different on each page, and the traffic to your site will be split evenly between the two pages. By running a test in this way, you'll be able to determine which headline performs better.

Once you have a positive result, you can either test another element, or try to find a new headline to beat the winning one. It's important, though, that you run any tests in isolation. Change more than one thing at a time, and you won't know which change contributed to the result. The one exception to this is if you're using a specific piece of software that can handle multi-variate testing.

## What You Should Test

Headlines:

When someone visits your website, you have just a few seconds to grab their attention. Often, the first part of your site they'll engage with is the headline. That is the first element you should test. By changing the headline, you can dramatically change the conversion rates. Get someone engaged enough to read your headline, and they'll want to continue reading more of your page. A benefit of testing a headline first is that you'll often get a result much faster because it is something that every visitor will see.

To create effective headline tests, you need to understand your customer and what their pain points and desires are. The headline should articulate what benefit they can get from reading further.

A simple shortcut for coming up with headline ideas is to look at what other competitors are doing in your marketplace. You'll likely find that there are different styles of headlines they use and different benefits they lead with. By making a swipe file of all these headlines, it will be easier for you to model them for your own business and test them.

The Offer:

After the headline, the offer is probably the next most important element to test. What is it you are selling, and what are people getting? Are they getting an e-book or a physical book? Are they getting information or actual coaching? How is the content delivered – all at once or over a period of time?

You can test how you structure your offer and see what works best. Sometimes people prefer digital products, whereas others prefer a physical version.

A perfect example is physical and digital books. My wife loves her Kindle, but I prefer to have a real book. They both contain the same content, but different people will have different preferences. You can always make both options available so that people can choose the one they prefer. In the online world, people have become used to instant gratification so you can even test providing both a physical version in the mail and an instant-access digital version.

Sometimes people don't want to buy a big course either, so you can test breaking your product into smaller sub-products. They may just have one particular need and a smaller, lower-priced product may be more attractive than a larger, more comprehensive course.

Once someone becomes a customer, it's a lot easier to get them to purchase something else from you. It could be better to have 10 customers at $10, than just one customer at $100. While the revenue is the same in both cases, the smaller price point means you're getting ten times the number of customers to market to again in the future.

On the opposite end of the spectrum, you can test creating a bundle of products. Bundle packages work well when you can say, "Okay, here's a three-for-the-price-of-one offer." And you take three of your courses and sell them for the price of one. Combining this with a limited-time promotion is a great way to convert more people into customers.

Language:

The language you use in your sales copy should be something that reflects the marketplace. Forums will give you some great insight into how your potential customers communicate with each other.

You want to ensure your sales copy is relatable to them. That way they will trust that you understand them and have a solution that can help them. As you go through forums, look for the type of posts with the most replies and/or the threads with the most views. Those posts are full of your hottest prospects.

Your competition will also be useful here. When you're studying the sales pages of four or five of your competitors, you'll start to notice patterns and themes that occur on most of their pages.

Go through their bullet points. If you find there's something that appears on every competitor's page, that's an indication it's something important to the market. Your product should also address this. If it's something that's not included in your product, find a way to address it, even if it means creating a bonus element specifically for that purpose.

A useful resource is the website AnswerThePublic.com. On this site, you can enter a keyword or phrase that relates to your market. In return, it will provide an extensive list of questions people are asking in relation to that topic. If you're ever stuck for content ideas, or the kind of questions you need to address in your sales copy, that resource gives you a huge amount of intelligent, useful data to work with.

When it comes to the language you use in your marketing, you should also consider the market sophistication. Different markets will be more mature (not in terms of the age of the prospect, but in terms of how established and educated that market is).

Take the weight loss market as an example. Fifty years ago, it would have been possible to sell a weight loss pill just by claiming something like, "New weight loss pill melts fat!"

Fast forward to today, and the market has seen those types of claims before. Now they're a lot more skeptical. A simple claim like that won't work anymore because the market has matured and become more sophisticated. If you wanted to sell a weight loss pill today, you would have to come up with a specific reason why that pill works. It will require a unique ingredient or mechanism, and the appropriate studies/proof to back up those claims.

Testimonials and case studies:

We've covered in previous chapters how important it is to have potential customers trust you. Testimonials provide an extremely powerful way to build that trust.

It's natural to have an inbuilt skepticism – especially when purchasing something online from a person you've never even seen. It often doesn't matter how great the product owner claims to be. People expect you to present yourself positively, so it may not lend much credibility to just tell them how awesome you are.

If you can get other people to do that on your behalf, you'll find it's a lot easier to build trust with your prospects. Even better is getting testimonials from people just like your ideal customer. Even with testimonials, many people won't believe they can achieve the same result for one reason or another. With a testimonial from a person just like them, it's much easier for them to believe in the product and their ability to get a result with it.

Case studies are one of my favorite types of testimonial because they are based on a real result from using the product. It's not just someone's opinion of how good the product appears to be. For really effective testimonials or case studies, you want to illustrate not just the result the person obtained, but also where they were before using the product. The result is not as important as the transformation.

To give an example, consider the various weight loss products that use before/after pictures on their site. It's one thing to see someone who is slender and toned, but without some context of what they looked like before, it's not as impressive. The bigger the transformation you can show, the more impressive the results will be.

When using testimonials in your sales message, use them at any point where you make some kind of claim about your product. People are naturally skeptical about claims. Immediately showing a testimonial that backs up your claim will go a long way in countering that skepticism.

Bonuses:

Adding bonuses to your product helps increase the perceived value of your product. A common objection from a prospect is that your product may seem too expensive for what you're offering. By adding bonuses, you help to alleviate that.

An important point on using bonuses is that you shouldn't add so many that they devalue the original offer. They should be used to complement your core product and provide something additional. While adding more value is usually good, you can add too much, so that your core product gets hidden.

A further benefit of adding bonuses is that it gives you some flexibility in terms of pricing. If you ever want to offer discounts, or a stripped-down version of your product, remove a bonus or two. You still provide the core content as a complete product, but it can be used to justify a price discount during special promotions.

Design:

The way your pages are designed also has an effect on your conversion rates. A 'pretty' site does not always convert as well as a plain website with minimal graphics. Designers often want to include lots of graphics, headers, and different colors. However, you may find that a plain website with black text formatted like an old-school physical sales letter works better.

Colors, and in particular the color of the headline, have also been shown to increase and decrease conversion rates. Red is often a color that shows an increase when used in a headline because it draws more attention.

Length of copy:

There's a famous quote about comparing the length of sales copy to the length of a woman's skirt – it should be short enough to keep you interested but long enough to cover the important bits.

Long copy can be effective, but long-winded copy should be avoided. A simple way to test the length of your copy is to start with as much information as you feel is needed. Then run split tests where you remove different sections of the copy, and see what impact it has.

If you find that removing a specific section leads to a decrease in conversions, then put it back in. You know that section is contributing to sales. You should even find ways to highlight it, draw more attention to it, and ensure people are reading it. On the other hand, if you find that removing the section increases conversions, or even has no affect at all, it's usually safe to leave that section out entirely.

Modality:

Going back ten years or more, when people first started selling online, the sales pages were purely text. Video was not a suitable medium to the internet. That's no longer the case now.

Video sales letters can get dramatically different conversion rates compared to text-based sales letters. They are not only a more visual medium, but they also allow you to control how the prospect is exposed to the sales message. With a text sales letter, a prospect could scroll to the bottom, see the price, and make a decision on whether to read the rest of the letter based on that alone. That way there's no way for you to build up the value and justify the price point. By using a video sales letter, the prospect isn't made aware of the price until you present it in the video. That gives you the ability to establish the value of the product first, so that there is less 'sticker shock' once they see the price.

Each market is different. There's no universal rule. I've seen products where a text sales letter performed best, and other markets where a video performed better. There are other products still where having both a video sales letter and the text sales letter below it has been the most effective approach. It's up to you to test what works for your product. But you should test.

Guarantee:

How long should your guarantee be? In a lot of cases, a longer guarantee period will lead to higher sales and lower refunds.

With a 30-day guarantee, customers are acutely aware of that time period. They feel like they need to hurry up and get some kind of result (or lack of) to make a final decision on whether to keep the product or not.

With a longer guarantee, many people forget about refunding the product after a while. They feel like they have a lot more time to evaluate the product. Before long they've forgotten about it, and your refund rate goes down.

Another benefit of a longer guarantee is that it shows more confidence in your product. That is particularly true if you offer something like a lifetime guarantee. It can help you get more customers purchasing the product in the first place. Again, it's helping to establish that trust.

One thing you can do here to build that trust even further is to use a 'guarantee testimonial'. That means you show an email of someone who asked for a refund and the reply where you provided it. It lets people know you stand by what you say and reassures them that if they do have a problem, they'll be taken care of.

If you're not comfortable with offering a long guarantee period because you feel people may abuse it, stop worrying. It doesn't happen. As mentioned above, typically, the opposite will occur. But one solution is to offer a conditional guarantee. Give people a year to claim the guarantee, but they need to provide some proof or reason to qualify.

For some products, I've offered people a double money-back guarantee. That shows I have huge confidence in my product and helps increase conversions. However, to avail of the double guarantee, they have to show they've followed the steps laid out in the product. I know if they follow the steps, they'll get results, so I'm confident about offering this. In the very rare chance they don't get results, the increase in conversions from such a strong guarantee will offset having to pay out the extra on the double guarantee.

You may find that some people just want a refund anyway, even if they don't use the product. In those cases, it's best to just refund the money they paid but not the extra amount you promised for action-takers.

Trials or Samples:

Depending on your product/service, you can test offering a trial or a sample to people. A good way to offer this is with an exit-intent message as someone is leaving your sales page.

It could be a free sample, or a free chapter, or even just a $1 trial. I've found that $1 trials can be particularly effective as a last attempt to convert a prospect. Even though they're committing a minimal amount, they're still making a purchase. Once they're in that buying mode, it's easier to get them buying more products.

One example is a product I sold for around $100. If people attempted to leave the sales page, they would be offered a $1 trial for access to the whole course, with the remaining split over two installments.

Not every trial stuck and converted into a full price sale, but some did – around 50% of all trials. More importantly, though, the $100 offer was just the initial offer. Once someone made a purchase – either at full price or at the trial price – they were offered an upgrade costing around $300.

Many people who took the $1 trial went on to buy the $300 upgrade. The trial buyers did have a lower conversion rate on the upsell, but this was all essentially 'found money'. Even if none of those trials converted into fully paid sales, I would have still missed out on all those additional $300 sales had I not offered the trial.

As a result, the $1 exit trial increased the overall revenue of that campaign by 55%.

<u>Live Chat</u>:

If you're looking to convert just 10% more prospects into customers, consider live chat. It's a way to deal with their objections while they're on your page.

It works particularly well for higher-priced products, where a prospect may be interested but have a question or a niggling doubt they need clarified. With a live chat option, you're able to address individual concerns before they have a chance to leave and forget about your site.

Interacting with customers directly and showing a real person at the other end will have a positive effect on your sales. When testing something like live chat, it's important to analyze any changes in conversion. You'll need to balance them with any extra time/money you're spending by having someone man the live chat.

To keep costs down, look at your peak order periods and just have someone available during these hours. Most businesses won't have the majority of customers purchasing at 3 a.m. so you won't need 24-hour availability.

One of my partners did something similar with a promotion of a higher-priced product. He didn't use live chat, but he did make himself reachable by putting his real phone number in the subject line of an email that said: "Questions? Call me – xxx-xxx-xxxx"

Some prospects did call him, and he was able to answer their individual concerns and get them to sign up. But more surprisingly than that, he also had many people who signed up without calling him. They later said the reason they felt comfortable doing so was that he was willing to be available if needed. They could see he was a real person and was willing to answer their questions.

Retargeting:

The past few years have seen new opportunities with the technology available to us as marketers and online business owners. One of those opportunities is in retargeting (or remarketing, as it's also known).

You've probably been exposed to retargeting, even if you're not aware of how it works. How many times have you visited a site, such as Amazon, and looked at a product without buying it, only to later find ads on another site promoting that exact product? That's retargeting in action.

With retargeting you're able to cookie each visitor that comes to your site. Later, ads on other sites around the web direct them back to your offer. It is an incredibly effective form of advertising because you are focusing on people who have already seen your offer. Rather than spending a lot of money to advertise to a broad audience, you show your ad to people that are highly targeted.

You can use retargeting to display ads that focus on different benefits and different angles, and drive them back to your site. They may have left your site for any number of reasons, but this gives you the ability to convert more of them into sales. In many ways, your retargeting audience is very similar to your email list of prospects. You keep exposing them to your sales message over and over. You may not convert everyone in that audience, but it can easily contribute to that 10% increase you're looking for.

<u>Streamlining</u>:

Finally, look at your whole sales process and see if there are ways you can streamline it or minimize any friction points.

One such example is your checkout page. Typically, if you're using a shopping cart, a customer will have to fill out multiple fields, such as name, email, phone number, address, etc., as well as their credit card information.

In many cases, there are fields you may not need, e.g. the phone number or company name. If you don't need them, leave them off the page. The fewer fields you require people to complete, the higher your conversion rate will get.

If your shopping cart has a coupon field that is displayed on the checkout page, consider removing it. The natural reaction of someone seeing a coupon field is to think there must be a coupon available somewhere. A significant percentage of people will then go and search for a coupon. The end result is that many of them will get distracted and won't come back. Or they won't complete the purchase because they think they should be able to get it cheaper. Independent studies have shown that removing the coupon field from a checkout page can increase checkout conversions by 10% or more.

## The Most Powerful Sales Tool

All the methods above can help to improve your conversions, but I've found that one method is more powerful than any other for getting people to take action.

Scarcity.

Introducing scarcity into your marketing creates a sense of urgency in your prospects. It's been shown that the perceived pain of losing something can be greater than the perceived pleasure of gaining something.

Used correctly, scarcity has the potential to increase your sales more than anything else. However, to quote Uncle Ben from *Spiderman*, "With great power comes great responsibility." Don't abuse it.

Probably the best example I could give on the power of scarcity is Black Friday. Once a year, you have people lining up outside stores at crazy hours just so they can save a few bucks on a new TV they don't really need. However, Black Friday is particularly effective because it combines two types of scarcity – time limited and quantity limited.

Not only are the sales just for one day out of the whole year (time limited), but many of the sales would be subject to stock levels too (quantity limited). When they're gone, they're gone. The best deals may not even last the whole day. That's why you see such a mad rush of people. If you can tap into just some of that desire for your own business, it's almost impossible to not increase your sales.

When it comes to an online business, adding scarcity into your sales process may need a little more thought. That is particularly true with a business selling digital products. With a digital information product, there isn't any reason why quantities would be physically limited. Likewise, the internet gives you the ability to sell 24 hours a day, seven days a week, so you don't want to hurt long term sales by making something too time limited.

For those reasons, a lot of online marketers will unfortunately end up using some kind of false scarcity, which ultimately hurts their sales. Fake countdown timers that reset with each page refresh or sales pages that say "only three copies left" of a digital e-book are examples of blatantly false scarcity.

It's perfectly possible to use real scarcity in your business, but you need to come up with a good 'reason why' to justify it. If you're selling a digital product, you have unlimited capacity. But if you're offering some personal attention to buyers, then you have a genuine limit based on your own resources. You can use that as your 'reason why' in your scarcity. Even though you could sell unlimited copies of the e-book, if you're giving some personal attention to buyers, you have to limit the number of people that get that deal.

Another genuine quantity-based reason could be that you're releasing a new product and want feedback from customers. You offer a discounted 'beta access' to a handful of people in exchange for their feedback. It's also a way to get testimonials in place for when you launch the product to the wider world at a higher public price.

For time-based scarcity, there are lots of reasons you can use. In this case, you just want to have a fixed time, e.g. 72 hours, where your offer will be available to people. After that, it's gone. It could be a discount, or a bundle, or a holiday special. Just make sure to take the offer away once it's finished. Don't be tempted to try and get a few more sales after the deadline. You may get a couple of extra short-term sales, but you'll damage your credibility in the longer term, especially if you plan to run these types of sales periodically.

Whenever you're running a promotion that involves scarcity, you'll get better results if you increase the frequency of communication as the deadline comes closer. That is something I've tested time and time again, and it always generates more revenue if you contact your prospects more.

For a typical 72-hour promotion, I may send out one email on the first day, two emails on the second, and three emails on the third day. As the deadline draws nearer, the increased intensity of the emails helps to nurture that sense of urgency. Another reason it works so well is that if people see '72 hours to go', they can easily put it off and say they'll purchase it later. But we know people are so busy that they'll forget about it after 10 minutes and may not ever return. By sending more emails in that last 24-hour period, you ensure your subscribers cannot miss the message.

One promotion using this method generated a 170% increase in sales by mailing repeatedly, compared to the sales from just mailing once about the offer. In fact, almost 50% of those sales came in during the last 12 hours of the promotion. Had I not sent those additional emails, it would have resulted in a lot less revenue. The truth is many people will wait until the last possible minute to make a decision. Using a hard deadline and reminding them of it forces them into making a decision. If you don't keep communicating with them, though, they'll forget about the offer entirely.

It's important to note that with the increasing frequency of emails, there's never any negative pressure involved. It's mostly just reminding them of the benefits of the offer and of the limited time left. If your product will help people solve their problem, then you owe it to them to make sure they are aware of it. Even more so if it's available at a discounted price for a limited time.

## How to Use Scarcity Effectively

Creating a campaign with scarcity can be as simple as creating a duplicate sales page with the discounted price, and then sending your prospects to that page. Once the promotion is over, you just remove the page and send people to the regular page. Simple.

You can find plenty of countdown timers online that you can insert into your sales page. While you can tell people the date/time the promotion will end, timers are great for visually demonstrating the scarcity and the time left. It gives your prospects a very real sense of urgency. The closer the timer gets to zero, the more likely it is to encourage your prospect to purchase.

The downside of this method is that it's not great for generating ongoing sales. You can only really run it once every few months. However, for my own business, and for my clients, I've developed an evergreen scarcity software that makes it possible to run scarcity campaigns on an ongoing basis.

It works by taking each new prospect through a sequence where the sales pages, emails, and deadlines are all dynamically customized for each person. Every lead goes through the same scarcity promotion, but the deadline is different for each person.

For example, if Bob joins on a Monday, his deadline date could be three days later, on Thursday.

If Jenny joins on Wednesday, her deadline date could again be three days later, on Saturday.

The key is that every component in the process is automatically and dynamically personalized for each lead.

Bob never knows Jenny has a different deadline. If Bob clicks on the sales page after his deadline, it will be displayed as expired for him, even though Jenny is able to view it via her link. Also, because the whole system is customized to each lead, the scarcity is 100% authentic.

In effect, it's like running a Black Friday sale every single day. Those are the types of campaigns I create for myself and clients. I probably don't need to tell you how powerful something like that is.

## Other Ways to Increase Sales

Use surveys to segment your prospects based on their responses and provide them with a more tailored sales message. If you're running simple multiple-choice surveys, you should give people the option to write out an 'other' response to a survey. You'll find that some people will write long, detailed messages as a response. They will be your hottest prospects (so you can consider following up with them personally). They'll give you a great insight into the pain points for your 'bleeding neck' prospects. Take this information and feed it back into your sales copy and into your email promotions so that you're addressing those pain points.

As an alternative to running a survey, just ask people to reply to your email with their biggest concern. Depending on your list size, that can mean you get inundated with replies. However, the personal interaction with your subscribers will always generate more goodwill with your prospects. (Getting people to reply to your emails is also a great way to increase your email reputation and ensure that more of your emails reach the inbox.)

As you use the surveys to segment prospects, create different sales processes to sell the same product. By creating a few different sales pages that highlight a specific benefit, you tailor each page to each segment.

Let's illustrate this with an example. Imagine you're selling a course teaching people how to get more website traffic from places like Facebook, Twitter, YouTube, etc. When you run a survey, you ask people which site they would most like to learn to drive traffic from. Then you segment them accordingly.

People who choose Facebook go onto one sublist. People who choose Twitter go onto another, etc. Now, when you send each of those people to a sales page, they are sent to one which has a headline focusing on a site that matches their response.

The people who selected Facebook may see a headline that says: *"Who else wants more targeted traffic from Facebook and other sites?"*

The people who selected Twitter may see a headline that says: *"Who else wants more targeted traffic from Twitter and other sites?"*

That simple example shows how you're focusing on giving people exactly what they're asking for. The more targeted you make the campaign, the better your results are likely to be. Any one of these methods could be enough to get you the 10% increase you're looking for in this section.

Another technique I've used to make more sales is to create 'hidden links' within a sales page. You take any element on a sales page, e.g. an exclamation mark in the headline, and hyperlink that to a special discount page. Any uninformed person visiting the page will never know it exists. But send an email to your subscribers and tell them exactly where it is on the page (or create a quick video showing it), and they'll be able to click through and get a secret discount. This works really well, especially as your subscribers feel like they're getting something just as a reward for being on your list.

If you want to make more sales and you're building a list of prospects, the best thing you can do is consistently send them emails. If you're constantly communicating with your customers and providing them with a way to purchase something from you, you will make more sales.

Even if you've exhausted your whole product suite and feel like you have nothing else to offer your subscribers, find relevant affiliate products to promote. You may not be getting 100% of the sale when promoting as an affiliate, but any additional revenue is something you would otherwise be missing out on.

PART 2

# AFTER THE SALE

## Chapter 4

# PRODUCTS

Now that you've acquired a customer, the hardest part is over. All that work will compound and bring you bigger gains from this point on.

This next section will give you techniques for generating even more revenue from each of your new customers.

The best time to make more offers to a customer is immediately after their initial purchase. Your goal is to find a way to offer them something that's relevant and adds more value. It should help them achieve their goals or solve their problems, quicker or with less effort. That can increase your immediate revenue, not just by 10%, but by many times that.

If you're stuck for ideas on what to offer people at this point, think of ways you can build on that initial product they purchased. To give an example from an information marketing product, the initial frontend purchase is often an e-book or a video training. Essentially, that is the manual or 'how to' for a particular technique.

A related upsell to that could be something which helps them implement the training in a way that gets them faster results, or results with less effort. That could be a set of ready-made templates, blueprints, or software that helps automate the tasks. It could be a coaching offer where you provide additional support. In this case, the upsell takes the role of a "do it *with* me" solution. An even more expensive upsell to that could be a complete "do it *for* me" solution, where you provide the customer with the finished product/result they're looking for.

I've covered the 80/20 rule already in this book, and again, it's something that holds true in this situation. You'll find that roughly 20% of your customers will make up 80% of your total revenue. Not everyone will buy your upsells, but you don't need them to. The 80/20 rule suggests that roughly 20% of your customers will buy something that is four times the original price. This assumes your offers are extremely relevant and provide the buyer with a clear advantage should they choose to purchase it.

For example, if we assume you're selling a $100 product, the 80/20 rule suggests that 20% of buyers would purchase something from you that cost $400.

With 100 buyers at a $100 price point, your frontend revenue would be $10,000.

With a $400 upsell, and a 20% uptake rate, that would be an additional 20 sales at $400, or $8,000 in revenue. An 80% increase from that one upsell alone.

But it doesn't stop there. The 80/20 rule holds true beyond just that first step. Of those 20 people who purchase the $400 product, another 20% would purchase an additional product at four times the price again.

In this case, that would be an additional four sales, but this time at $1,600 apiece. An extra $6,400 in revenue, bringing the total to $24,400.

Compared to the $10,000 frontend revenue, that's an additional $14,400. That gives you a 144% increase, by simply adding two additional products into the funnel.

We could go further and say that 20% of those customers would buy something four times higher still. In this case, that would work out to 0.8 people buying a $6,400 product.

In reality, you can't have 0.8 of a sale, but it could be one person buying a $5,000 coaching package or similar. Over time, as you get more buyers, the fractional numbers would approach those whole numbers. (Following the 80/20 rule, you'd need just 125 buyers to get one buyer of your highest-level product.)

A $5,000 sale would take your total revenue up to $29,400.

That is from only 1% of your buyers taking this highest-level offer.

A single $5,000 sale is a relatively small amount in terms of actual buyers. However, that one coaching sale would generate the same revenue as 50 frontend sales.

This extra revenue can be a great way to leverage your affiliate program. If you know you've got a strong backend in place, you can pay more commissions to your affiliates. In turn, they'll send you more customers,

A lot of the increases we'll talk about in this section will give you much more than the 10% goal we've been going for so far. That is why we spent so much time on the first three chapters.

Due to the compounding nature, any small increase in those three areas will be amplified dramatically with the larger increase we can get in this chapter alone.

I'll include an example below to demonstrate just how powerful the compounding effect is.

Consider our base numbers as below. For simplicity, we'll use round numbers and assume a 10% conversion at each point.

10,000 visitors

↓

1,000 prospects (10% of visitors)

↓

100 buyers at $100 (10% of prospects)

↓

$10,000 revenue

If we have a 10% increase in each area before considering the upsell, we'll see it change to:

11,000 visitors (10% more than before)

↓

1,210 prospects (11% of visitors)

↓

133 buyers (11% of prospects)

↓

$13,330 revenue (33% more than before)

At this point, we've realized a 10% gain in three areas.

Rather than just a 30% increase, it's compounded to 33%. Perhaps not that big of a compounding effect, but consider what happens when we introduce the upsell sequence above.

If we implement the first $400 upsell and have 20% of buyers (133 customers) take that, we'll have 26 buyers at $400. That's an additional $10,400 in revenue taking the total of the second funnel to $23,730.

By getting a 10% tweak in the first three areas and adding the first upsell, we have a 137% increase in revenue.

That is where the power in this process starts to become apparent. The key is that you can't be afraid to offer more products to people.

You don't necessarily have to structure your upsells according to the 80/20 rule of saying it should be four times higher. Find a range that works for you, your customers, and your market. Just don't be afraid to sell something higher priced, or at the very least, something else.

One of the very first upsells I used in one of my digital product businesses was a ~$100 upsell on a $10 product. The upsell was 10 times the price. With that offer, approximately 10% of all buyers would take the upsell. Immediately after adding that, I'd doubled the revenue of that offer. Needless to say, I was happy with doubling the revenue overnight. I also kicked myself when I realized how much revenue I'd missed out on before adding it.

On top of that, I also created a downsell, which was a 'lite' version of the main upsell. That was offered for ~$50 to people who declined the $100 offer. That converted a further ~10% of all buyers. At that point, each $10 buyer would generate on average an extra $15 in immediate backend revenue for a 150% increase.

Another example was a higher-priced product that was $500 on the frontend. This offer converted well, but I knew there would be a way to generate more revenue with an upsell after purchase. For this particular offer, I created an additional $500 offer (so the same price as the frontend) and was able to convert 40% of all buyers. Looking at the stats, you can see this upsell wasn't as effective in terms of increase as the one above, but a 40% increase is still 40% more than I had originally.

Different marketers will use different approaches in their funnels. Some prefer to offer products that are lower in price than the original product, as those will get a higher conversion. This is true, but it's important to consider the actual dollar-per-buyer you generate, rather than just the conversion rates.

For example, a 10% conversion on a $100 product ($10 per buyer) is better than a 35% conversion on a $25 product ($8.75 per buyer).

The other important benefit of starting with a higher-priced product is that it leaves you room to offer a downsell. You'll get people taking the high price point regardless, but what about those that don't? When you offer a downsell at a lower price, they're much more likely to purchase, as they've been price anchored to the higher price. The lower-priced offer seems like better value in comparison. If you start low and they decline it, it's almost impossible to get them to then take a higher-priced offer.

If you're not comfortable offering a stripped-down version as a downsell product, or if it's not practical to do so, you can also break the offer down into a payment plan. That can work equally well. Instead of dropping the price from $100 to $50, simply break the $100 into three payments of $35. Often, this can convert at a similar rate as a regular downsell. If someone completes all the three payments, it actually equals double the revenue of a $50 downsell.

As you'll see, there are no hard and fast numbers to use with this. You also don't need everyone to purchase the additional upsell to still achieve very substantial gains, even with a modest uptake on the upsells. Getting at least a 10% increase in revenue from your existing customers following these methods is virtually guaranteed.

## Using Technology to Maximize Sales

During the whole upsell process, you want to make it as easy as possible for your customers to say 'yes' and minimize any friction. You do that by structuring the offer so that it's appealing, but you can also use technology to maximize your sales by making it easy.

The first method is through the use of one-click upsells. Typically, when selling online, you'll have people go through a checkout process where they have to enter their billing details, credit card information, etc. When presenting them with upsells, you'll get a much higher conversion rate if they don't need to fill in all that information again.

Many shopping carts will allow the use of one-click upsells. Those enable customers to simply hit one button to add additional products to their orders. In those cases, you need to be very clear with customers that clicking the button will add the purchase to their order. If you don't, you'll get angry emails and chargebacks. But using one-click upsells will typically increase conversions because it's easy for the customer to say yes.

Another way to present an upsell is simply as an additional item offered on the checkout page itself. Those 'bump' offers can be added where the customer simply has to check a box to add it to their order. For the best results, it should not be something expensive that needs a lot of copy for it to be sold. It should be something simple and appealing that people can add to their cart.

Imagine the confectionery stands in a supermarket. Those are perfect 'bump' items. You're standing in line waiting to check out, and you see a magazine or candy bar. As a small, impulsive buy, you don't think much of adding it to your order. On the other hand, if you're going in for bread and milk, and they have a $500 TV for sale, that's not something you're likely to add to your basket.

Giving people a deadline to take advantage of an offer will also help you generate more sales of the upsell. You have a couple of options here. The first can simply be a countdown timer that starts as soon as customers complete their initial purchase. Once it expires, the special offer is no longer available. We covered scarcity in the previous chapter and, as mentioned there, seeing that timer get closer and closer to zero is a strong motivator for a lot of people to take action.

The other option is to make the page strictly a one-time-only offer page. That means there's no inherent time limit, but as soon as they leave that page, it won't be accessible to them again.

You can easily test either method and see which one performs better for your customers. For the countdown timer method to really work, you don't want to give people days to decide. Typically, no more than an hour or so, or a day at the very most. Some people may not like that kind of time constraint, so you may find giving them more time to examine the offer makes sense. But in this case, make it so that once they leave the page, it's gone forever.

Your upsell pages should include a link where someone can decline the offer so that they don't feel forced into a purchase. The upsell should always be optional. However, when creating your "no thanks" link, you can include some copy that will at least get customers to consider your offer objectively. For example, if you're offering them a heavily discounted done-for-you solution as an upgrade, your "no thanks" link could say something like:

*"No, thanks. I'd much rather do all the hard work myself or pay an extra $500 later."*

Psychologically, that will have an effect. Clicking that link is admitting the statement is true. Nobody wants to spend more than they need to, or work harder than they need to. At the very least, if someone has scrolled to the bottom of your upsell page to decline the offer, something like this can make them think twice about the offer. It can also be used to reinforce the benefit of purchasing the upsell. In this case, the benefit is that the hard work is done for them, and it's done $500 cheaper than normal.

Of course, you don't have to make your upgrades limited in any way. It's perfectly okay to just present them with your other products at full price. This way you're just making them aware of something they otherwise may not have been. If there is no time constraint on the purchase, then you can always make an offer in other ways. Transactional emails and follow-up emails can remind them of any additional products if they decline initially.

Look at Amazon and how they always offer additional products to their customers after purchase, but it's never done with any kind of time constraint. They'll offer the "frequently bought together" items on the main product listing page (which is similar to the 'bump' method). Then they'll also show you things like "customers also purchased", a selection of products they feel are relevant to you based on what other people have purchased. If you're ever stuck for ideas on what to try in your sales funnel, study big sites like Amazon. They'll rarely be doing something unless it's making them more money.

## How Many Offers Is Too Many?

You'll have to establish this for yourself. A good guide is to start with just two or three additional offers after someone has made a purchase. You can always offer more products later on in the relationship through email marketing. But introducing too many upsells at the point of purchase can have a negative effect.

I've literally seen some marketers offer more than 10 products in one go, one after another, all before the buyer could get their original purchase. The customer had to sit through each of these extra presentations, wait to find the 'no thanks' link, only to be faced with another one. As you can imagine, that product got a lot of negative feedback and a much higher refund rate than would normally be expected.

Remember, your goal is to help your customer solve their problems. If you're offering five or more different items all at one time, it will probably overwhelm them rather than help them.

If you've ever purchased anything from GoDaddy, you're probably aware they're quite aggressive with their upsells and add-ons. Personally, when I buy a domain, I just want the domain, but it's clearly working well for them. They'll often bring people in with a low-priced product as a loss leader, and then generate a profit on that customer from selling the additional products on the backend.

You should never, ever create an upsell that is essential for the frontend product to work or function correctly. If a customer has purchased something from you, they've put their trust in you, they've got their credit card out, and they've sent you money. If they then get to the thank you page and there's an offer saying, "Well, this product really doesn't work unless you buy this extra component here," it will have a really negative impact.

It's like going to a car dealer, buying a car, but then finding out the wheels will cost you extra. The car is essentially useless unless you pay more. The initial product should stand alone, on its own. They should be able to get the results they want, the results you've advertised. The upsell should just be a way to get those results faster, or with less effort, or through automating a process.

## What If You Only Have One Product?

Finally, let's talk about what you can do if you only have one product. Ideally, you should have more, and if not, you should at least be working to create more.

In the meantime, it doesn't mean you can't generate any extra revenue from your customers. The easiest thing to do is find relevant affiliate offers you can promote and collect a commission on. Again, the product should be something that will help them reach their goals faster. Don't just promote something purely for the financial incentive.

Adding some element of scarcity may be more difficult in this scenario. As an affiliate product, it's probably available to the general public to purchase at any other time. However, if you have a good relationship with the vendor, you can see if they would be willing to offer discounted access in return for you sending all your new customers to them. In this case, you can usually create a page that includes some scarcity, because the only way they can access the discounted page is through you.

I was able to build a whole business by providing a backend affiliate offer to a lot of product creators in the information marketing space. Many of them would have lower-priced offers, up to around $100 or so, but very few would have anything at a higher price point.

I created an evergreen webinar that sold a $2,000 product and made it available to these product owners to promote. We split the profits on any sales. It was a way for them to generate additional revenue without needing a high-ticket offer of their own.

Even though the $1,000 commission was less than the $2,000 they would have received if it had been their own offer, it was easy to use. It also didn't require them to invest the $100,000 or so needed to develop the offer in the first place. They're getting all this additional revenue with virtually no extra effort (aside from adding one link to their thank you page). Their customers get some valuable bonus content on the webinar, and my team handles all the product fulfillment and customer support.

## How to Make $1,000+ per Hour

We touched on coaching earlier in this chapter. Getting paid to share your expertise is something that can be extremely lucrative. A single $5,000 coaching client could bring in the same revenue as hundreds of customers buying low-ticket $10-$20 items.

Not only is it a great way to directly generate more revenue, but having a premium option will also help customers see the relative value in what you have to offer. Even if they don't take the premium option, the standard option looks like good value.

As the saying goes, if you want to sell a $2,000 watch, put it next to a $10,000 watch and it looks reasonable. If you put it next to a $200 watch, then it looks expensive.

Same watch. Different context.

Coaching is something that can be applied to almost any market where you're selling results based on the application of information. People with the means to afford it will pay for the speed, convenience, accountability, and sometimes even just the identity of being able to afford a high-priced offer.

However, coaching is something a lot of people are hesitant to do, and understandably so. If your goal is to create more freedom in your business, you don't want to be tied to coaching clients.

In those cases, a group coaching program can bridge the two ideals of having more money but spending less time in your business. With any kind of coaching you're likely to find that there are some fundamental principles you'll teach to all of your students.

With a one-on-one coaching program, it would be extremely time inefficient if you were to teach the same materials over and over again. But in a group coaching program, you can structure the training in such a way that you have a pre-recorded training that covers all the fundamentals. Then you follow that up with weekly calls with students where everyone can get their questions answered in one go. The actual time spent on coaching is minimal since the bulk of the workload is now taken care of by the pre-recorded materials. You only have to spend an hour or so per week attending to all your clients' needs.

One of the clients I've worked with has a 12-month coaching program set up in exactly that way. The students get all the training, which is drip-fed automatically to them over a fixed period, so a new lesson is unlocked each week. Then once a week, he has Q&A calls with his students where they can talk about any problems they're having.

Anyone who can't make the call can submit their questions via email beforehand and get the recording of the call the next day. That way all the students get to hear answers to other questions that may not impact them now, but could be relevant later on.

By structuring the coaching in this way, it is less likely for the students to be overwhelmed, since the materials are broken down into small chunks. It's easier for them to follow along with each part of the process and, ultimately, get results. For students who follow the training, my client has a 100% success rate. Obviously, there are people who do nothing, but that's true of anything, whether it be people who purchase business coaching or a diet book.

The important point to take from this is that for an hour a week, he can serve all of his clients. When you consider that each student could be worth as much as $5,000 to him, spending one hour a week gives a massive return on the time spent.

Consider just 100 students in a year at $5,000 – his revenue from the coaching would be $500,000. Even if he spends two hours per week delivering the coaching (let's use 50 weeks in a year for simplicity), his hourly rate over the year would be $5,000 an hour. Not bad. There are probably very few, if any, other activities in your business that can yield that kind of return on your time.

## Building a Coaching Program Into Your Business

If you've never created a coaching program before, the easiest way to do so is to start with a small 'beta' group coaching. Teach all the parts live and have each student on each coaching call. As you go through the content, you'll be able to get immediate feedback on how well it makes sense to each of your students. That will ensure it fits their needs to give them the solutions to their problems. Make sure you record each of your sessions.

Once your live coaching is complete, those recordings form the basis of your pre-recorded training that you deliver in your ongoing group coaching program. In many cases, you may be able to use the exact recordings from the live calls. Most likely, you'll take those and re-record them from scratch while implementing the feedback you received. It sounds like a lot of work, but it's important to remember you only have to do this once.

You then use the same recordings to automatically deliver coaching to every student you take on after that. If it takes you 20 hours to record all the fundamental training, that saves you 20 hours for every new student you enroll because you won't have to cover the same material with them personally again.

Your coaching program doesn't have to be a $5,000 program that lasts for 12 months. Plenty of coaching programs out there are only six to eight weeks long. You can still do those in the same group coaching method. Or for those shorter time frames, you may want to include more one-on-one coaching. It really all depends on what makes it easy for you to help your customers get results. When it comes to pricing the program, remember to think of the value it will bring to the student, and not how much time you will need.

## Sell More by Repeating Yourself

Following the idea of creating content once to use over and over again, there is also nothing to stop you from running promotions more than once. If a particular promotion works well when you run it, then it is still likely to work well in another year, or another six months, or even another three months.

As you build out your follow-up sequence, you'll be able to see what kind of lifetime your leads have. You may be getting a high percentage to open and click your first few emails, but after 90 days, the numbers will typically be a lot less. Over time, your leads will become less and less responsive.

A lot of business owners think they can't send the same emails to their list more than once, ever. The truth is that if you send the same promotion even 90 days later, you are likely to be tapping into a whole new audience. Even the leads who were exposed to it before may not remember it. Most autoresponders will have some form of automation that automatically segments buyers onto a new list you create. So you can easily send this promotion again to all your non-buyers while excluding those who purchased already.

If you can run the same promotion four times a year, I guarantee you will sell a lot more of that product. You'll also increase your productivity by not having to create a whole new campaign four times. When you have a few tried and tested campaigns that you can repeat every few months, you'll be in a position to run a special promotion every month of the year. That 10% increase for this section should look pretty easy now.

Chapter 5

# PRICING

In this chapter, I'll show you how to use pricing as a tool for increasing overall revenue in your business. There is some crossover with chapter three, in that this can also be used as a tool to increase initial purchases, depending on the types of test you run. Typically, a pricing test is something you'll want to focus on *after* you have sales coming. You need to be generating customers to test which price point works best. That's why I've kept it in this section.

As far as pricing goes, it's not just about how high or low the price is. It's more about how customers perceive the price and the relative value. You can change the customer's perception in different ways depending on how you position your offer, even if the price stays constant.

To start, we'll consider how simply raising or lowering your prices will affect your overall revenue. Sometimes a lower price point works better, as it will typically generate more customers. As we've seen before, once you get customers into a buying state and get them to make that initial purchase and commitment, it's a lot easier to get them to purchase more things from you.

Having a lower price point may not result in any revenue increase on the initial frontend. A $10 product that converts at 10% produces the same initial revenue as a

$20 product that converts at 5%. However, in the first scenario you'll have double the number of customers. That gives you more people who see your upsell sequences and a more valuable asset in terms of a bigger buyer list.

Depending on your existing product suite, it may even be worth it to test removing the non-paying prospect part of your funnel and to simply focus on transforming people from a non-paying visitor to a low-ticket buyer of $5-$10.

Conversely, raising your price points can increase your revenue. In many cases, you'll find that if you raise your prices significantly, your visitor-to-conversion ratio may drop, but the increased revenue per customer can negate any impact from that.

There's a famous example in Robert Cialdini's book *Influence*, where a jewelry store owner was having trouble selling a particular set of stock. Before leaving, she scribbled a note to her sales assistant telling her to change the price on the stock so that it was ½ the regular price. The sales assistant misread the note and marked the jewelry at twice the regular price. Surprisingly, the stock all sold because people equated the higher price with a sign of quality. In this case, sales went up, and profits went up too.

This story illustrates that people will often pay more than you think they will. Depending on what you're offering, it may even be more beneficial for you to have fewer customers at a higher price. That in turn can lead to fewer overhead and staff costs, which will increase overall profitability. Even if revenue stays the same, this reduction in expenses can mean your pricing structure gives you more profits.

There are plenty of examples of pricing experiments, but it's something you'll need to test in your own business. Just because someone else does it, it doesn't mean it's the right thing for your business.

You also need to be aware of the effect this has on a macro scale. For example, an increase in revenue on the frontend can look good. But if the bulk of your revenue comes from your backend sales, you need to consider that too. If you're reducing the number of customers who go through your funnel, then that may have a negative effect on the value of each visitor coming to your site. It's vitally important that you're able to analyze this objectively. If you send 100 visitors to page A and 100 visitors to page B, which page generates more revenue throughout your funnel, and also throughout the typical lifetime of a lead?

## How to Start Price Testing

To begin, just start with small increases and see if conversions drop off. We've seen how the jewelry store owner doubled her prices and sold lots more of her product, but such a large initial increase is not something I would recommend. Our goal with each section here is to look for the small improvements first. It's best to start with increasing your prices by a smaller amount of 10% or 20%.

There are a couple of benefits to this gradual scaling approach. First of all, we're hitting our target if we can increase the revenue by 10% with just a simple 10% increase in price. Secondly, you'll often find that with such a small price increase the effect on your conversion rates will be negligible.

One of the disadvantages of doubling your price is that your conversions will drop and you'll have fewer customers going through your funnel. With a smaller price increase, it's possible to maintain conversion rates while extracting more revenue. Start price testing by slowly increasing the price in small steps while monitoring the conversion rates.

While the conversion rates remain steady, everything else in the funnel is likely to remain steady too, and any increase on the frontend price is likely to be a pure gain. Once you find the price point at which conversions start to drop off, that's a good indication you've reached a tipping point. Though it may be possible to keep increasing prices and offset the conversion drop with the extra revenue, at this point, you need to be much more aware of how the whole funnel is performing. Keep it simple. Start by raising prices by 10%. If conversions look good, move on.

Whenever you're testing prices, you also want to ensure you're using software that will not only allow you to track accurately, but also show the same price point to returning visitors. If you have a $50 product and are testing a $40 and $60 price point, you don't want someone who purchased at $60 to later see the $40 price point with no difference in the actual product. A customer never appreciates that. Most split testing software will have an ability to serve the same page to the same visitor on repeat visits.

## Adding in More Options

Up to now we've discussed simply raising or lowering the prices of your existing product. Adding more options to your sales page can increase the revenue. The simplest way is to add a premium option to your page. You'll find that there will always be people who choose that option. Those sales can often be a lot more profitable than the standard price product you offer. It could be for no other reason than that they like being able to identify as someone who can afford the most expensive option available. If we're honest, nobody needs to spend $5,000 on a watch when a $5 watch will do pretty much the same job in terms of telling the time. Someone who can afford the $5,000 watch isn't just buying it for its ability to tell the time. They like buying expensive things.

Not only will you typically increase revenue from having people purchase the premium option, but in many cases, it will change the perception of the value in your lower-priced products and make those look more reasonable. Going back to the watch example mentioned earlier, a $2,000 watch next to a $200 one looks expensive, but put it next to a $10,000 watch and it looks a lot less so.

The other main benefit of including a premium option is that you have to sell a lot less to make the same revenue. Selling one watch at $5,000 is typically not harder than trying to sell 1,000 watches at $5 each. Not only that, but the overheads and support involved in dealing with 1,000 customers will eat into the profitability of that second scenario.

When including premium options in your business, consider offering those price points to your customers up front. Starting with a high price point like this, and then dropping down to lower-priced products, will often mean you pick up those premium buyers first. Then the people who can't afford that will take one of the lower-priced options. If you offer everyone the lower-priced option first, you'll invariably sell to some of the premium buyers who would have otherwise purchased something more expensive from you.

To illustrate that with an example, a partner of mine was selling a high priced program through a webinar. It was doing well. When looking at ways to maximize the revenue, we came up with the idea of adding a smaller offer right after someone registered for the webinar. That can be a very successful strategy, but it's important that the offer you make at this point does not compete with the offer you will make on the webinar. It should complement it, yes, but not compete.

My partner's program was sold at $2,000, $3,000, and $5,000 for various levels of access. He also had some other training which covered the fundamentals provided in his coaching (albeit without any personal interaction). He decided he'd offer the recordings as the post-registration offer for ~$50.

The $50 offer converted well, but what happened was that the conversions on the main webinar offer dropped dramatically. The reason was that, although the offers were vastly different in terms of depth of content, they were too similar in terms of the topic. So people who purchased the $50 offer didn't feel the need to get the $5,000 coaching. They figured they could give it a go on their own first, rather than pay 100 times more for the personal coaching.

While adding more offers to a funnel usually means more revenue, this is one situation where adding a new offer had a detrimental effect. Some people who would have chosen a $5,000 coaching program now only spent $50 with him.

If you plan to offer a premium price point to your customers (and you should), make sure you offer that option up front, or alongside your regular price point, so that they can decide what to take. If they decline that, then you can offer the lower-priced option.

## Price Anchoring and Decoy Pricing

The example of my partner above is a perfect illustration of the effect of price anchoring. That is the value a customer places on something based on how they've been exposed to similar offers in the past. Nothing is inherently expensive or inexpensive when taken in isolation. You need something to compare it against.

Where my partner was offering a $50 option up front for recorded training, people were anchored to that price point. When it came time to offer his $5,000 coaching, which covered a similar topic, the price anchoring of $50 meant that people considered it expensive.

On the other hand, if he had led with the $5,000 price point, people would have been anchored at that price point. He could have offered the same course he sold for $50 and put a $500 price tag on it. Even though it would cost 10 times more than what he had originally sold it for, compared to the $5,000 coaching, it would still seem a lot more reasonable. Hence, it would have resulted in a lot more revenue. The premium buyers would have taken the full coaching first, and a certain percentage of the other customers would have taken the $500 package after.

Another famous example of price anchoring is an experiment with *The Economist* magazine and how they structured their pricing for subscriptions.

In a study, an advertisement was shown to 100 MIT students. They were asked to choose which option they would subscribe to.

The three options were:

Web only access – $59

Print only access – $125

Web + print access – $125

At first glance, the middle option looks completely redundant. After all, who would willingly pay the same price for less stuff?

If that was the case, why not remove it? The answer is that the second option is doing a very important job of anchoring the price. It is there to provide a value that can be used for comparison.

84% of people said they'd take the web and print option, 16% would take the web-only option, with (perhaps unsurprisingly) none taking the print-only option.

The same question was put to another 100 MIT students, but this time the print-only option was removed. This time, the results were staggeringly different: 32% chose the web and print option, while 68% chose the web-only option.

Consider the potential revenue from these two sets of 100 people. The first example with the three pricing options would give $11,444 in sales. Removing the print-only option and the second set of 100 people would generate $8,012 in sales.

Simply including the third option resulted in a 42% increase in revenue, even though nobody purchased that option. It was simply a decoy price that served to anchor people to the value of the print option.

Without that option, people were looking for the cheaper option – they were in bargain seeker mode. Once they saw the value of it, though, and realized they could get more 'stuff' for the same price, they became value hunters, and that took precedence.

One thing to consider if you're in a market with a lot of competitors offering the same things is that you can be drawn into a pricing war. If your competitors are offering products at $100, you may feel that you need to have a lower price point to offer more value. More often than not, this just results in a race to the bottom where you're equating value with price, driving down prices, and trying to provide more value.

The smarter tactic is to set yourself apart from the competition so that there is no way to compare. Once you're the only one in the market, you cease being a commodity.

A simple example is to find a way to make your product or service unique, even if you provide the same product and service as others.

For example, why can Starbucks charge $3 for a coffee that others can sell for $1? It's because they created an experience around going out for coffee. The experience is what differentiates them. Changing the perception of what people were purchasing allowed them to create a new category for themselves.

Context is also important in how much price elasticity you can have. A beer from a local cafe or bar might be half the price of what you'd pay in an upmarket hotel in downtown Manhattan. You'd expect to pay more for your beer at the Ritz, even though you could get the exact same product elsewhere.

## Reframing Your Prices

If you have a particularly expensive product or service, reframe that price point to make it seem more affordable.

A $1,000-a-year subscription product is only $85 a month, or a cup of coffee a day. You're not changing the product, or even the pricing, at all. You're just helping your customers perceive the relative value they get.

Once you break that value down into smaller amounts, the relative value increases.

Similarly, if you're selling something like a $10,000 coaching package, that is a considerable investment to make all in one go. Reframe that price point by telling people they can spread the cost with a credit card, and the payments will only be $300-$400 a month. Not only does it seem a lot more affordable, but it's also a lot easier to imagine getting a return on a $300-$400 investment each month. Again, nothing in the product or pricing has changed. The change is in the perception of value on the part of the customer, and also the value they perceive that they'll get from it.

When someone buys something, they're looking for a solution to their problem and want a return on whatever they're spending. It may not necessarily be a monetary return, but it's important that they can see the value. If your $10,000 coaching package means that a customer will free up an extra 20 hours of working in their business each month to spend with their family, then you can equate the value to that. Would $300 a month be worth an extra ~250 hours of freedom a year?

## Using Shipping Costs to Test Pricing

If you sell any kind of physical product in your business, you can test how you use the shipping charges to increase conversions. More and more people these days expect some kind of free shipping. One of the highest reasons for shopping cart abandonment online is that people get to the checkout page and are hit with unexpected shipping charges. It can be either charges that are too high, or simply having any kind of shipping charge.

Again, this goes back to price anchoring. If someone is purchasing a product for $100, that is the price anchored in their mind. Once they check out and see a $10 or $20 shipping charge, the price they have to pay is higher than what they were expecting. Bye-bye customer.

Try increasing your initial prices to $120 and give them free shipping. Now, when people go to check out, there are no surprises. The total price they have to pay is the same as the price they were anchored to. What's more, you can put a monetary value on the free shipping and tell them they're saving $20 with your free shipping offer. Now they feel like they're getting a discount.

The overall price they pay doesn't change. The net profit to you doesn't change. But in the second scenario, the customer is much more likely to complete the order.

I've seen similar results with authors who sell their books online using a launch model. They'll often say, "Get the book for free, just pay $7.95 shipping." Others will say, "The book is $20 on Amazon. You can get it for $7.95, plus we'll include free shipping."

Those are identical offers. The net cost in both cases is the same. Even though it's the same offer, the perception on the part of the user can often be quite different and give other results. Something as small as that could give you the 10% increase in your sales that you're looking for in this section.

Again, this is something you should test, since the initial price increase may harm 'add-to-cart' conversions slightly, but the decrease in cart abandonment may more than make up for this. You can't assume the result by what you think people should go for rationally.

To show you just how irrational people can be in this respect, I can give an example of my own. I grew up in the UK. When I moved to the US, I found it strange to learn that everything was sold at a certain price, but then sales tax was added at the checkout till.

In the UK, we have VAT, which is similar to sales tax, but it's always included in the listed price. If you see something listed at £100, then you pay £100. However, when I moved to Washington State, they had a 9% sales tax. If something was listed as costing $100, it cost $109 when you went to the checkout.

Even after living there for several years, it would annoy me and even catch me out (like trying to pay for a $1 item with a $1 bill, but having to then break a $20 because it was actually $1.09 and ending up with a pocket full of change). I'd much rather know the full price up front so I can make an informed decision. A lot of your customers are the same.

## Displaying Your Prices

How you physically display your prices can also impact conversions. Have you ever noticed how a lot of restaurants, especially the more expensive ones, won't include the dollar sign next to the price? They'll just include the number. They've tested it and found that people are inclined to spend more if they see numbers without dollar signs. It may be completely irrational, but that's not the point. If it works and makes them more money, they'd be stupid not to do it.

In addition to displaying their prices that way, many restaurants will also place one of their more expensive items towards the top of the menu. This is where your eyes naturally fall first. Again, this is to anchor you to those high prices so that the rest of the items below it look much more reasonable. They know most people won't go for the extravagant option, but as we've seen, they don't need people to – it's just there to compare the relative value of everything else. Some people will order the expensive option anyway, just because they can, so the restaurant wins all around.

When it comes to displaying your price, there are several ways to change the perception of that price from the user.

Let's take the amount of $1,499.

It can be written as follows:

A - $1,499.00
B - 1,499.00
C - 1,499
D - 1499

In the first example, A, we're including the dollar sign and the cents. As we've learned from the restaurant industry, including the dollar sign can have a negative effect on the sales. Plus, including the cents makes the number appear physically longer. Subconsciously, a longer number appears to be a bigger monetary amount.

In example B, we've removed the dollar sign, but the number still appears quite long.

In examples C and D, we've removed the cents, but D has also removed the comma. That has the effect of being a slightly shorter number, but the other effect is more subtle.

When you see a number written as 1,499, your brain 'speaks' that out as one thousand, four hundred, and ninety-nine. A relatively long number.

On the other hand, 1499 can be read as 'fourteen ninety-nine'. It's a much shorter number when read out loud, but also as you read it out in your head. The shorter number sounds like a smaller monetary amount to our subconscious.

The difference on the page is subtle, but it can produce a statistically significant difference in conversions. Any potential difference, however small, is not to be ignored.

If your product consists of multiple elements, it can also be beneficial to display a value, or separate price, for each individual element. Typically, the sum of all these individual elements will be greater than the price you're selling the product for. That can help demonstrate the overall value of your offer.

For example, if you're selling a product for $1,000, it may consist of 6 different parts that would sell for $300 each on their own. The total separate value would be $1,800 in this case. The full package price of $1,000 again represents good relative value compared to the sum of the individual parts. If you don't display these individual values, your prospects may not have a way to easily establish the value of what you're offering.

## Breaking Your Own Pricing Barrier

Sometimes the most limiting factor in setting prices is not what the market will bear, but what you feel you can justify charging. In many cases, the market will happily pay considerably more for what you can offer. If you're selling your own information or expertise, then it's easy to undervalue what you have to offer.

When I first started in the information marketing business over a decade ago, I was afraid of charging anything for my content. Having never done anything like this before, I wasn't sure that (a) people would pay me for my knowledge, and (b) if they did pay, that they would even like what they paid for.

As a result, the very first information product I created was something I gave away for free to build a list. Then

I monetized that list by selling affiliate offers and other products I had licensed. Those licensed products were products other people had created, and I purchased the rights to sell them as my own.

Even though I knew my product was perfectly good because it was based on actual methods and I was using it to generate an income for myself, I still had that fear. I thought, "What if people don't think it's very good?", so I was afraid to charge for it.

When I eventually got over that, I started selling $10 products, then $100 products, and up to $500, $2,000, and now the much larger revenue-sharing, coaching, and consulting services. But at each point, it took a mental leap for me to give myself permission to charge more. Once I raised my prices, I found that people were perfectly willing to pay those prices. The only reason I hadn't made that much before was down to my own internal fears.

A secondary benefit to raising my prices was not only being able to physically charge more, but also to work with fewer customers/clients while maintaining revenue. One client at $5,000 is ultimately a lot less work to support than 500 customers of a $10 product.

On an overall profitability outlook, it would probably take 700-800 customers of a $10 product to generate the same profit as one $5,000 client. If you consider the support and overheads that go into dealing with 500 customers, those costs would eat into your profits.

If you're struggling to justify increasing your price point, particularly because of fear, focus on the value you bring rather than the actual cost of the product. For my own business, I try to make things as automated and efficient as possible, and I use templates and systems to help me work quickly. That means the overall time I personally have to spend on a task may not be very substantial. As a result, it can be hard to justify the price I'm charging if I'm only looking at the time it takes me to complete a task.

However, consider that it's taken me over 10 years of education, research, and hard work to get to this point. Then even more time to build the processes to implement the knowledge I've acquired. When you compare the time and money it would cost someone else to learn what I've learned, then it is much easier to justify the value in what I'm offering.

As an example, you could be charging $5,000 a month for consulting. On the face of it, charging $60,000 a year may seem like a huge amount to ask. But if that helps a business owner generate an additional $600,000 in revenue for their business over the course of the year, then it's a bargain price. Even if you only help someone double their investment, it's still extremely valuable to them.

Remember, nothing is expensive or inexpensive by itself – the price is only there to compare its value to something else.

Once you understand the value you can bring to someone, it's much easier to get over that fear of pricing your product or service too low.

## How Higher Prices Help Your Customer Get Better Results

As we mentioned earlier, raising your prices can help you sell more because people will associate a high price with a sign of good quality. We've all heard the saying, "You get what you pay for." That framing holds true for many people. Some people just don't like to purchase something that seems too cheap because they feel it won't be of a high enough quality for them.

The truth is, the content I provide in a $20 book may be fundamentally similar to the content I would provide to a $5,000 consulting client. There is obviously some more value in the personal contact and the accountability involved in the coaching. But often, the people who become a $5,000 consulting client don't want a $20 book that they have to read and try to implement themselves. They want someone to help them and know that they'll be more likely to get a result. They know if they were left to do it on their own, then they would never follow through.

By spending a large amount, their mindset becomes, "I've invested a lot in this. I have to make it work." They will get the work done, and then be able to get results, which is what you want for your customers.

I'm sure everyone reading this book has more than a couple of books they've never finished, let alone implemented. I'm also certain there are people who purchased this very book and never made it to the point where you are now. (Well done, you!)

However, it's rarer to have someone spend thousands on a coaching program and not at least go through the training. If you're selling information that helps your customer solve a problem, then getting them to consume the information is essential to them seeing results.

Personally, I want to work with individuals who are motivated and who are likely to get results. The people that are willing to invest the most in a solution are the ones who are most likely to end up getting their desired result.

As an aside, I've also found that the customers who only purchase cheap products take up disproportionately more of your time and resources in terms of support. It's been my own experience, and one I've confirmed with many other partners. Someone who purchases a

$10 e-book is a lot more likely to want more personal interaction, faster results, and for the smallest amount of work possible. What's more, when they don't get the instant results they're looking for, they're the first people to go and cry, "Scam!" anywhere they can online.

I remember a time when I was just beginning to build my own business and I had sold a product to a customer who needed some help using it. In his case, the help wasn't that he couldn't use the product. He just didn't want to spend his time figuring out how to do it. He came to me saying unless I could help him use it, he wanted a refund. At this time, I was still studying in university and every $100 sale was a big deal for me, so I did everything I could to make sure I didn't lose it.

Fast forward to six weeks later, and I'd been responding to a new helpdesk ticket from him pretty much every day. I was doing things way beyond the scope of his initial purchase, but I was doing it out of fear of losing that sale. In the end, he told me he decided the product wasn't for him and he requested a refund anyway. Looking back now, the amount of time I lost was worth significantly more than the $100 he paid me. And at the end of it, I didn't even have that.

For me personally, raising my prices was a way for me to minimize that kind of negativity in my business. It ensures I only work with more positive people who appreciate what I have to offer. People who are willing to take personal responsibility for the results they get from any training or consulting they purchase.

In turn, those clients at a higher price point will get better results. Once they do, they'll give you better testimonials, which will in turn help you sell more of your products.

## Chapter 6

# PERSISTENCE

At this point in the process, your business should already be performing substantially better. You should have more traffic, more prospects, more customers, and more revenue from those customers. In this section, we'll look at how we can generate more long-term revenue from customers after they've finished their initial purchase. While you can create new products to offer, a more efficient method can be to create a product or service they are happy to pay you for over and over again, in the form of a continuity program. That will provide you with predictable, reliable income every single month, even if you were to fail to bring in any new customers.

At the most basic level, it could simply be a monthly membership where customers pay a small amount of money every month in return for some new content, e.g. a newsletter. At the other end of the spectrum, it could be a more complex software solution that customers use on an ongoing basis, for which they pay a monthly fee to retain access.

Software lends itself very well to a recurring program, as it's something your customers will use often. It also typically requires costs on your part for updates and maintenance, so the monthly service charge is more acceptable to customers. But regardless of what avenue you take, the customer should be getting ongoing value in exchange for their ongoing payments.

## What to Offer in Your Recurring Program

Starting with a continuity program can often be daunting if it's not something you've built into your business plan, or if you don't have a clear idea of what to offer. While a software product may lend itself to a recurring payment, it can be more difficult to come up with ideas for a purely content-based program.

One of the simplest programs to create is a newsletter in which you provide more content on a monthly basis to your customers. It can be something you send via email, or an actual, printed newsletter. From my own experience as a consumer, I much prefer printed newsletters. I'm more likely to consume them, and when I consume them, I'm more likely to remain a subscriber. If it's something delivered by email, I often don't read it for months at a time because it's not urgent. Then I find myself thinking, "Why am I still paying for this if I'm not reading it?" and cancel.

The great thing about creating a newsletter is that you're being paid to create content for your business. You're guaranteed to generate income from the work you put into it. When creating a new product to sell, there's always that thought of, "What if this doesn't sell well?" But if you know 100-1,000 people are guaranteed to pay you for the next newsletter, it's a lot easier to stay motivated and create that content. Predictable income is always good.

You don't even need to create a lot of content up front. It will often be enough to have the first issue completed to send to new subscribers, and then you create one a month. Stay engaged with your customers and ask them what their main issues are. Their replies will give you ideas of what to cover in future issues. Then it makes sense that, if you're constantly providing what they want, they'll stick around.

There's a trap people fall into when creating content for a subscription model. They feel they need to include more and more content to keep people happy and prevent cancellations. Often, the opposite is true. It's better to have two or three pieces of actionable content/advice people can use and get a result with, rather than throwing so much at them that it overwhelms them. If there's too much for them to consume and use, they're not getting the most value from it. If they don't get value, it's unlikely that they'll want to keep paying.

You might think you don't know how to come up with a newsletter every month, or with enough new content to justify the fee. Consider something like a CD or DVD of the month club, where you simply interview someone in your marketplace and deliver that to your members. All you need to do is sit down and interview an expert in your market for sixty minutes, and you have an instant product that you could send out on CD or as a downloadable MP3. Get it transcribed, and you have an instant, printed product to go along with it.

It could take you no more than a couple of hours a month to fulfill. It doesn't require you to have any expertise yourself either. You're leveraging the knowledge of other people, and at the same time, you're becoming an expert by association. A lot of people are happy to do these interviews, particularly if you give them the ability to promote their business. Let them mention one of their own products in the interview, or provide a website address people can visit for more information.

You can also create an affiliate program for this offer. Ask each interviewee if they'd be willing to share the offer with their subscribers and give them 50% of the monthly sales on an ongoing basis. Over time, as you have more people interviewed, you can have more people promoting your continuity program.

Another model for a simple continuity program is to add a paid community aspect, for example a forum or closed Facebook group. People like to interact with other, like-minded people. Those types of communities are great at fostering goodwill. In many cases, it will turn out that your customers are creating all the content themselves, as essentially each member becomes a contributor. It may take some initial effort on your part to jump-start conversations, but after a while it will grow organically and members can all help each other out.

## When to Offer Your Recurring Program

A great place to make an offer for your continuity program is your upsell sequence. Once someone has made that initial purchase from you, we know they're likely to purchase something else from you. It is often difficult to try selling a subscription-based product on its own. Many people will be wary of getting into a long-term contract or committing to regular payments. However, you shouldn't be afraid of taking advantage of the lowered resistance during the initial sales cycle by adding a recurring element as an upsell.

As it's difficult to get people to commit to a monthly payment plan, you want to make it as easy as possible for them to agree to it. When placing the recurring product into the upsell flow, you can take advantage of the technology to provide a one-click upsell. All they need to do is add it to their order with a single click, and they'll keep getting billed every month with no further interaction needed.

Compare that to a scenario where you're trying to sell a subscription on the frontend. People have to physically get their credit cards and fill out all the details to commit to a monthly purchase. It's easy to see why adding it as a one-click upsell works well. There are also payment processors that have relationships with card networks to automatically update your customer's card details when they are issued with a new card. Stripe.com is a payment processor I've used with this feature. I wasn't aware of the feature at the time, but I was pleasantly surprised to see how the card details were always kept up to date without the customer having to re-enter any information to keep the subscription active.

You're not restricted to offering a recurring product in the upsell flow of your business. Plenty of companies go directly for the recurring sale as their frontend product. Similarly, others promote the product further along in their follow-up sequence. Finally, there's no reason you can't offer it in more than one place in your sales process.

## What to Avoid When Selling Continuity

When you're selling any kind of continuity- or subscription-based service, you need to make sure your customers are aware of the monthly charges. Several years ago, there were marketers who would just have a single line in their long sales letter that mentioned something about the customer being billed $97 a month after 30 days. Other than that one line buried in sales copy, the customer was unaware they were signing up for a product with a recurring element. Why would they do that? Because they knew if they were extremely transparent about it, then their conversions would drop dramatically. Instead, they decided it was easier to hide the details and bill the customers later. Many of those customers would be completely unaware of the charges.

It got to a point where the FTC had to step in and release a series of guidelines on how to sell continuity products. You have to make sure you're very clear that people are signing up for a continuity program and they will be billed in the future. That means you can't hide the details somewhere in the middle of the sales copy. Instead, the terms of the program should be listed clearly, in a sufficiently sized font, next to the order button. There should be no ambiguity about the fact they're agreeing to sign up for a recurring purchase.

Similarly, when it comes to offering a continuity program as an optional add-on, or 'bump' item, you cannot check an agreement box during the checkout process by default. If the continuity is added to the order by means of something like a checkbox, then it has to be unchecked by default and the user has to consciously check it themselves.

Understandably, a lot of people reading this will say being transparent with customers is just good business practice. That's true. Unfortunately, not everyone feels the same way, so these rules were brought in to help deal with those marketers.

## Getting Quick Recurring Revenue

If you don't yet have a product or service you can sell as a continuity program, then look at products you do have. If you have higher-priced products, you can simply offer those with a payment plan as a way to generate some additional revenue.

To someone who may not be able to afford a $5,000 coaching program, you could offer access for $500 a month instead, to make it more manageable for them. With the group coaching method described earlier, the extra workload from having one more person on a weekly Q&A call is minimal.

Alternatively, you could consider another price point of $300 a month just for the recordings of the coaching content and the recordings of the Q&A calls. That option leaves out any live interaction, but it gives you another way of generating some revenue on an ongoing basis. Moreover, it requires zero extra work on your part.

Using an example from my own business, I had a digital product that sold very well to my own list for approximately $500. However, there were people emailing me saying they couldn't afford it, even though they wanted to purchase it. After the initial launch period was over, I sent out a survey to those who didn't purchase it. I asked them if they'd reply with the main reason they didn't invest.

Overwhelmingly, it was because they didn't have the funds to purchase it during the small window that it was available. A couple of days later, I re-opened the offer for 48 hours and sold it only with a payment plan of six payments.

The result was that it generated almost 2.5 times the number of sales compared to the initial promotion. It's important to note that in this case I didn't expect all the customers to complete all six payments, but even if every customer only completed the first payment, that would still be an extra 42% revenue boost – just because I offered the payment plan afterwards. In actuality, it worked out that 50% of all payments on the plan were completed. This gave a 125% revenue increase compared to the initial $500 standalone offer.

There are a couple of points in this example which I want to highlight. When I did the re-opening, I was careful to engage my subscribers in conversation first. I asked them what they needed from me in order to be able to purchase. They told me they didn't have the funds.

When I then re-opened the offer with the payment plan, it was positioned as me helping them. I was simply giving them what they'd asked for, i.e. a way to make it affordable. It didn't come across as a money-grab exercise on my part. The result was that I had subscribers thanking me for making it available to them this way.

Secondly, I was very deliberate in that the initial launch of the offer only had the single, full price point available. In my experience, if you offer people a payment plan up front, you'll make less overall. Plenty of people who are able to pay the full price will take the payment plan if it's available. A percentage of those will cancel and not complete the full term, thereby reducing the average customer value.

By only making the full price option available initially, you make sure anyone who can afford the full price pays in full. That goes back to the earlier statement about starting with a high price point to convert the premium buyers first, then the lower price point will convert the rest of the buyers. Also, the price anchoring of the high price makes the payment plan amount seem a lot lower in comparison.

You want to make it easy for people to say yes to your offer, so offering a trial might be something to consider too. Trials often have a relatively high conversion rate. The downside is that they'll also have a much higher cancellation rate and a higher rate of failed payments going through. If you want to use trials, be wary of those aspects and don't assume that each free trial, or $1 trial, will turn into a guaranteed ongoing payment.

Trials are definitely useful, but they're one of the last things I would use. One of my offers sold a physical product with two payments of $97 ($97 up front and $97 after 30 days). There was also a version that sold the same product but with a $7.95 trial to cover shipping, and then two payments of $97 (so $7.95 up front, $97 after 30 days, $97 30 days after that).

The trial generated a much higher conversion rate in terms of visitors-to-sales. However, the actual revenue per visitor was only around 30% of the version where they paid the first $97 up front. In the case of the trial offer, only around 20% completed the first payment, and even fewer completed the second payment.

When offering these options side by side, it was clear that one was losing money. To reposition this, I made the upfront payment the only option available to customers. If they decided to leave the page and dismiss that up-front payment, then they were presented with the trial as an exit popup 'downsell'-type option. This maximized the revenue per customer, since those who could afford the $97 up front took that. Then others, who were not initially convinced, could still take the trial after. Even though only 20% of the trials converted into a rebill, that was still 20% more revenue than just having one option.

## Maximizing Recurring Revenue

Once someone subscribes to your continuity program, the best way to maximize your revenue is to ensure they stick around as long as possible. There will be people who cancel, but your goal is to maximize the average stick rate of your customers. There are several effective ways of doing that.

Pain of Disconnect:

You can create a 'pain of disconnect' that will arise from them canceling the subscription. That means the very thought of not having access to your product/service causes them some kind of emotional discomfort.

A perfect example is a cell phone. It's something you pay for on a monthly basis (which is for all intents and purposes a continuity program). For most people, the thought of not having a cell phone would cause them huge discomfort.

You want to replicate that same feeling in your own program. While it's unlikely you'll have a service as essential to someone as a cell phone, the more important it is to them, the less likely they are to cancel.

With something like a software solution, the pain of disconnect may be more obvious, in that if they cancel, they lose access to it. They may also lose any data they've acquired during their membership. However, for something like a newsletter, it can be more difficult to instill that same feeling. That is why, if you're selling something simple like a newsletter, it's useful to have some kind of community aspect to your program that is dependent on being a paid member. Once people get invested in a community, they're more likely to want to maintain access, even if they can do without the actual newsletter.

I use lots of tools in my business that would have a huge pain of disconnect. The most obvious examples would be my hosting account and autoresponder account. Without the hosting, I'd be unable to sell anything online. Without my autoresponder, I'd have no way to communicate with the thousands of people on my email lists.

I gave the example earlier in the book of how I built my first autoresponder using a free service. Then one day, the person running it decided to shut it down unexpectedly. For me, there was a very, very real pain associated with the closing of that account. If you can find a way to generate that in your program, you'll have a very successful long-term business.

Dealing With Cancellations:

There will always be people who cancel, but you can take certain steps to at least generate more revenue from those customers.

The simplest way is to try to 'save the sale' in some way. Either by offering access to another product of yours (that may be worth the equivalent of three to six months' membership) or by offering to give them a special discount rate. You may not want to give them discounted full access while charging other people the full price, but you can come up with a 'lite' version that still has most of the main benefits, while being ~50% of the costs.

Sometimes, people may just need a break to use the funds for more important things in their lives. If your shopping cart has this ability, you can offer to 'pause' their membership for a period of time and reactivate it later, rather than cancel outright.

Using 'Churn' to Your Advantage:

The churn rate in a subscription business refers to the percentage of people that cancel each month. You need to have a firm grasp of your numbers. For anyone with a recurring program, churn rate is the most important.

If you're selling a product and you know your average customer will remain for four months, you can easily increase revenue by trying to sell 'bulk' subscriptions at more than the price of those four months.

For example, let's look at a program costing $50 a month ($600 a year) with an average subscription lifetime of four months. That means each customer is worth $200 on average. You can easily offer a yearly plan for the rate of $300. That represents a substantial 50% discount on paying 12 months at $50.

Some people will take this option because of the relative value it offers. As we've seen previously in the pricing module, by having the ability to compare prices, some people will go from 'bargain seeker' to 'value hunter'.

Even though you're discounting the price by 50% to the customer, you're actually *increasing* the customer value by 50%. It goes from the average $200 customer value up to $300. You're putting more money in your pocket by charging them less.

However, it's important to emphasize that for this strategy to work you need to know your average stick rate. If your average customer stays for eight months, offering them the deal above would cost you money.

<u>Grandfathering the Rates</u>:

If you're just starting out with a subscription model, you may want to offer a lower rate for the first 100 or so subscribers. As a 'reward' for them becoming an early adopter, you can grandfather them in at a lower cost. If you plan to sell a service for $100 a month, let the first 100 people join at $50 a month and tell them they'll be guaranteed that rate for life. If they do later want to cancel, remind them it will cost them twice as much to rejoin in the future.

When presenting a recurring offer as an upsell, use a discount as a 'reason why' you're making that one-time offer to them. For an upsell to be really effective, it should be a special offer with a limited-time discount. Giving them a 50% lifetime discount if they subscribe then works well.

Serialize Your Service:

Serializing the service is possibly one of the most effective ways to increase retention rates. That works particularly well if you find you have a low average number of rebills. You may not want to be constantly creating new content month after month, year after year, if your average customer only subscribes for between three and six months. In that case, it may be more efficient to create a fixed-term continuity program that is just 12 months long.

Instead of everyone getting the same issue each month, they start with issue one the month they subscribe and get issue two the second month, etc. The key to making it work is numbering each issue, e.g. "issue 1 of 12". Then they know there are 12 issues in total.

People don't like to leave sequences incomplete. By giving them a definite end date, and labeling each issue, you make it more likely for them to want to complete the set. The closer they get to completion, the stronger that desire is. It's similar to the pain of disconnect mentioned earlier.

You'll find that people will rarely get to issue 10 out of 12 and then quit, when there are just a couple of months left. It would cause them discomfort to be missing those last two issues. Without a definite end point, however, there would be no negative impact for them if they unsubscribed.

Since each person always gets issue one at the start, it means if people cancel and want to get back in later, they have to start over from the beginning of the sequence. There's a clear incentive here for people to remain a subscriber.

Giving Bonuses:

Providing unexpected and unadvertised bonuses works extremely well for improving retention rates on subscription services. If someone sends you a gift, then the law of reciprocity compels you to do something for them too. In this case, it will often mean that you decide not to cancel the subscription, or at least not right away. Perhaps it's the British side of me, but I'd feel incredibly rude if someone sent me a bonus and my response was to accept it and then tell them not to charge me anymore.

Look at the main drop-off points in your membership and pre-empt those with a bonus. If you find most people cancel after four months, then send them a bonus with the third month's payment. If possible, make the bonus have a greater value than the subscription payment. Remember, the value doesn't have to come from what it costs to produce, but it comes down to the value it can bring to the user's life. If you're able to provide high value with a digital bonus, then your fulfillment costs are zero.

Reselling Your Existing Subscribers:

I've mentioned Ben Settle in this book already. He is a genius when it comes to subscription-based services. Not only is he great at getting people to join his monthly newsletter, but his main skill is reselling the membership to his existing subscribers.

Every month before the latest issue of his 'Email Players' newsletter comes out, his emails talk about some of the specific tactics and strategies he's sharing in the next issue. However, he also keeps his current customers on the same list as prospects. As a customer myself, I'm getting all of these same emails. The result is that I get just as excited about what I will receive. If I had any doubt about whether I wanted to continue getting the newsletter, then his emails quash it completely. In fact, in my entire business, that is the only subscription payment I'm actively happy to see go out. Once it does, I know I'll soon have that newsletter delivered to my front door.

Make Past Content Available:

If your subscription model is based around a new piece of content each month, you'll end up with a lot of content that new subscribers have never seen before. One way to make use of it is to create a back catalog of all the previous issues and offer that to subscribers as well. Either charge the full price for each individual issue, or bundle them together at a discount.

This is all content you've already created. It doesn't cost you anything extra to produce it, so you can leverage your previous efforts to get more revenue this way. If you have a year's worth of past content, present new customers with a one-time offer to get all 12 previous issues for the price of three. That will give you an instant boost in revenue without any extra content creation on your part.

Micro-Continuity:

Want to make more by charging less? Micro-continuity programs could be the way for you. A micro-continuity program is, as the name suggests, based on a small monthly payment, which could be as low as $5 a month.

For that amount of money, you don't need to give people a lot of 'stuff' to justify the subscription fee. It could just be a short report each month, or access to a community/forum, and that's it. But because the cost is so small, people will keep paying for those types of programs for a long time.

In many cases, for those who do want to cancel, it's almost too much hassle to go and find a way to cancel a $5-per-month subscription. Many other people won't even feel or notice the difference that $5 a month makes to their account. On the other hand, a $100 charge may need a lot more justification in their mind to keep it going.

I've promoted products as an affiliate that have had a micro-continuity element attached to them. For some, I've had people paying for it five years after the initial promotion. Consider that most programs costing ~$100 a month barely get three months' worth of rebills. A $7.95 monthly charge that someone keeps paying over five years yields more revenue in the long term. Obviously, in this case, cash flow could be an issue if you're paying for traffic and counting on the revenue to offset the advertising. As a backend offer, it gives you potential for a very reliable and steady income stream. It's also significantly easier to convert customers into a $5-a-month program than it is to convert them into a $50-a month-program. Typically, the higher the price point, the more aware they will be of the value they're getting for it, and the more they'll need to justify the ongoing cost.

Finally, the longer you're able to keep them subscribed, the longer you'll have their attention and be able to send them emails for other offers.

## The Perfect Continuity Program?

Back when I was about 10 years old, I saw a commercial on TV for a new magazine that came with parts to build your own model T-Rex. Each month, you'd get a new issue with new parts, and at the end of it, you'd have a complete model.

I remember going to the newsagent, and the first issue was just 50p. For my 50p I got the magazine and the first few parts of the T-Rex skeleton – in this case, it was the skeleton of the whole T-Rex head. In the magazine were all these interesting facts about the T-Rex and a picture of what my finished model would look like when complete.

I was hooked.

The next month came around, and I couldn't wait to get the next issue. Only this time, the price was higher. Apparently, the first issue for 50p was just the introductory price, and the regular price was $2.99. Still, I got some new parts to the model and another magazine.

Over the next few months, I kept buying the magazine (after all, I'd started it, so I didn't want to end up with half a T-Rex) but quickly found my enthusiasm waning. The magazines weren't as interesting as the first issues and truthfully, I was only really buying it now for the pieces of the model. Some months it was just a rib bone. I'd pick up my issue and think, "Is that it?"

Before long I really didn't want to keep spending my money on the magazine, but the closer my T-Rex got to completion, the more determined I was to finish it. I knew if I missed an issue, I'd never be able to complete it. Even though I didn't want to keep spending money on it, I was still hounding the newsagent to make sure they kept a copy aside for me behind the counter.

Eventually, the model was finished, and I was happy. Kind of. I was glad to have completed it, but I also knew that in total it had probably cost me $100. In all honesty, if I'd seen that model selling in the shop for $100, there's no way I would have purchased it.

From a marketing perspective, there were some things the magazine company did extremely well. They had an attractive offer for their target market (a 10-year-old boy). They had a very low barrier to entry (but only for the first issue). They provided a lot up front (if they'd gone with just a rib bone for the first issue, I wouldn't have come back). And they serialized it with a definite end point (so the closer I got to the end point, the more I wanted to keep paying for it).

However, looking back on it now, the thing that stands out most for me is that the value wasn't there. When you're selling something to your customers, they should be getting more in value than what they're paying you.

I knew the model that cost me $100 would cost no more than $20 in the stores. In the end, I couldn't help but feel a little taken advantage of. It's probably no surprise that I've not purchased anything like that again, and have actively discouraged my own son from doing something similar. A happy customer would not only buy more from the same company, they'd also be more likely to encourage others to do the same.

# PART 3

# PROFITABILITY AND PRODUCTIVITY

**Introduction to Part 3**

The final section of this book will focus on the final two profit multipliers – profitability and productivity.

These aspects are less tangible than the techniques in the previous two sections. The improvements you get in the next section may not be immediately apparent, but that's not necessarily a bad thing. There is perhaps more leverage in these sections than those that go before them.

The final four chapters are all closely related, and the concepts of profitability and productivity have a lot of crossover. Rather than combining them all into one giant chapter, they are presented here in separate chapters following my L.E.A.D. pattern. Longevity. Efficiency. Automation. Delegation.

## Chapter 7

# LONGEVITY

When creating your products to sell, consider what kind of shelf life a product will have. If you're creating an information product, there will be a certain time period for which the information is relevant. For markets like weight loss, the fundamentals are always the same. You'll teach people how to eat less, eat healthily, and move more. There may be different methods and variations of eating/exercise, but the fundamentals will be the same in 20 years' time.

On the other hand, if you're creating a product that is dependent on technology, it may be obsolete within a year or less. A perfect example is any type of information product that teaches people how to do SEO, or search engine optimization. Google makes hundreds of algorithm adjustments every single year. If you create a course on what works today in SEO, the same may not be true in a year from now.

When creating a product like this, don't make something that needs constant updating. Every time you have to make an update, it will cost you an investment of time in your business, and your time has a dollar amount attached to it. Creating a product that's valid for five years, compared to one that's redundant after a year, gives you a huge productivity boost. It may not be something that's immediately quantifiable, but over time the gains are there. Admittedly, creating a product that will last five times as long may take a little more work, but it's unlikely it will take five times as much work.

Continuing with the SEO example, there are courses that will often claim to exploit a particular loophole or glitch in Google's ranking algorithm. They teach that by using this, people will be able to rank their sites and generate as much free traffic as they need. Those loopholes may indeed work for a short amount of time, but the problem with loopholes is that they are prone to being shut. Once Google updates their algorithm, the course is obsolete.

The better course to create would be one that focuses on teaching the fundamentals of good SEO. That is mainly creating great content that genuinely helps people, and building links to that site by promoting it in places where your audience may find it. That process has worked since Google's inception and is likely to continue for many years to come. It's aligned with Google's purpose of providing the best, most relevant content to its users. While there may be occasional updates to processes, the fundamentals around good SEO are likely to remain the same. A course built on those fundamentals will have a much longer shelf life compared to anything built on exploiting loopholes.

## Work Once, Get Paid For Years

Jeff Walker has mastered the idea of creating a product with a long shelf life with his Product Launch Formula training. Jeff has been successfully selling his course for well over a decade now. While he has refined and updated the methods, the fundamentals behind it have remained the same.

Building a product like that doesn't just help with your productivity, but also with your promotion. All the efforts you put into marketing your product will still pay off five years down the line. If you're creating a new product every single year, then you need to come up with a new marketing campaign for every single product.

If you stick with the same product, rather than replacing it, any promotional efforts you put into it the next year will amplify what has gone before it. It also lends more credibility to your product when people can research it and see that you, and the product, have been around for a significant amount of time. In that time, you're also likely to have many people posting results online. If you research Jeff's product, you'll see literally millions of pages in the search results talking about his product, and many, many customer testimonials spanning a decade. That kind of credibility and social proof is almost impossible to build up if your product has a short shelf life.

My whole goal with this book is to teach you how to compound small gains into larger ones. This idea is no different. With all things being equal, if you were to put that same time and energy into constantly promoting one product, you'd find that product would still have better results than the sum of five individual products. When trying to push a car that's broken down, 90% of the effort goes into moving it that first inch. Then it has momentum. Any additional effort you put into moving it will help it go faster. If you get it moving and then put on the handbrake, it would take you a lot more effort to get it moving again. That's exactly what happens when you try to constantly create new products once your old ones become obsolete.

## How to Future-Proof Your Products

You can future-proof your products by carefully considering what information you're including during the content creation phase. The more you focus on the fundamentals, the more you're likely to protect yourself from having excessive updates.

Even with the best preparation in the world, it's inevitable that sometimes you'll need to update your product, or at least parts of it. To minimize the amount of updating, break down your product into discrete steps or modules, and create a separate piece of content for each.

People respond better to information that's more organized. If any content does need to be updated, simply update that particular module rather than the whole course. That also holds true for any new content you may want to add to the course. Simply build on those additional modules as and when you create them without having to redo a huge part of the product.

The product is only relevant for as long as it helps your customers. Don't be afraid to get their input on what works for them, and what kind of results they get from using your information. You may find that there are sections people struggle with. Pre-empt any future customer service problems by creating another piece of content to address those specific concerns. If you've taken a modular approach to your content creation, then it's easy to just slot this extra piece of content into the appropriate place within your product.

The overall benefit of creating products that stand the test of time is that it gives you more time to build your business, rather than manage it. With this additional time you can instead create a whole new product that caters to a different audience in your market. Or perhaps a new product that solves a different problem for your current customers. Rather than recreating that single product every year, you could instead have a whole new product every year to add to your funnel. By adding higher-priced products for existing customers, you'll increase overall revenue.

## Chapter 8

# EFFICIENCY

We started this book by talking about aviation. The industry is a great example of how you can improve efficiency by examining all the parts of the business in extreme detail.

There's a famous story of how, in the 1980s, American Airlines were able to save roughly $40,000 a year in costs by simply removing one olive from each first-class meal. It doesn't sound like one olive would do much. When you compound that over thousands of flights a day, over millions of flights a year, however, it adds up.

Another example is fuel. Fuel is the most important operating cost for an airline, so they are always looking at ways to reduce that cost. Northwest airlines estimates that for every 25 lb of weight saved, the company saves almost half a million dollars a year.

It's surprising what many different airline companies have been able to do just by focusing on making their planes as lightweight as possible. Some use special paint to prevent microscopic bumps on the surface. This helps to reduce drag, and therefore, fuel usage. Other airlines save 300-400 lb by keeping their craft with a polished metal livery rather than painting them. Even the toilet usage is examined to ensure they're not carrying more water than necessary.

In this chapter, the goal is to find ways to be more efficient in running your business. That will enhance the overall profitability of the business. For a moment, I want you to forget about trying to make more sales, adding more funnels, or any of the activities we've discussed previously. All of those measures will undoubtedly generate more revenue, but right now, I want you to imagine that you can't do any of those things. You can't create any new content, you can't create any new products, and you can't do anything to drive more traffic. However, you can still find ways to increase the overall profitability of your business.

It's worth mentioning again that you won't be able to do any of this unless you have tracking in place. You need it to cut out all the waste in your marketing and advertising. Even if you're using free traffic methods, certain sources will give you a better return on your time than others. To improve the profitability, you need to understand which ones work best so that you can cut the waste.

Look at the 80/20 rule again. We can assume that about 20% of your advertising efforts will be bringing you about 80% of your results. To improve the profitability, we want to hone in on that 20% and cut out the rest. While it may sound counter intuitive, you can have a more profitable business by cutting out 80% of all your advertising spend. You may have a lot less revenue as a result, but revenue alone doesn't pay the bills. Profit does. To illustrate this point, let's use the example below.

Imagine you're spending $500 on advertising to bring in $1,000 in revenue.

For simplicity, we'll assume this example is selling a digital product, so that costs to fulfill that $1,000 of sales is negligible.

With $1,000 in sales, you're making $500 profit from $500 in advertising.

That's not a bad result at all. I'm sure any company would be happy to see those kinds of numbers. But the truth is that it's not as good as it could be.

The 80/20 rule suggests that 20% of that ad spend ($100 out of $500) will generate 80% of the revenue ($800 out of the $1,000).

Conversely, it suggests that 80% of the ad spend ($400 out of $500) will generate just 20% of the revenue ($200 out of the $1,000).

Cut out the bottom 80% of advertising sources, and you end up with an ad spend of just $100, but revenue of $800.

Your revenue figures are lower: $800 compared to $1,000.

But your overall profit is higher: $700 compared to $500.

This is just one example of how cutting the waste gives you a more profitable business.

## How to Find the 80% to Cut

You'll need to get more granular with your tracking. It may not be enough to consider which medium works well. Consider what specific sources in that medium, and what subsections of that source, work best.

Advertising in newspapers would be a broad advertising strategy. But use specific coupon codes, or advertising URLs, within each publication, and you'll see which newspapers are getting the best results.

Getting more granular with that, create a unique coupon for each day of the week. Not only do you weed out the poor-performing newspapers, but you also refine your campaign to only advertise in the best newspapers, on the days that bring in the best results.

Getting more granular in your advertising and targeting like this can mean the difference between a winning campaign and dismissing an entire medium altogether.

Looking at newspaper advertising as a whole, you may find that it's not profitable and dismiss it as an advertising platform entirely.

Looking at individual newspapers, you might find that advertising in the best newspapers means you break even on your ad spend. In that case, it might be worth continuing just to be able to generate buyers at no up-front cost.

Looking at which days perform well, you may find that you can cut out half of the days that are under performing and making a loss. You turn an otherwise losing, or break-even, campaign into one that consistently turns a profit for you.

This same kind of day parting works with Google AdWords and Facebook advertising too. You can get even more granular down to the specific time of day that your ads run. Typically, during daytime hours people are at work, so less responsive to your sales message. You may find that it's in the evening when they're home, and when the kids are in bed, that they're more likely to buy from you after clicking on an ad.

Google AdWords allows you to target people based on the specific keywords and phrases they enter. It's important to note that with AdWords you can also target by 'broad', 'phrase', or 'exact' match keywords. The same keyword can yield vastly different results depending on which of those you target.

Broad match keywords will display your ads to a larger audience, but it may be a lot less targeted. Consider using a keyword target of 'luxury cars'. On a broad level, your ad may display to people who type in 'fast cars' or 'luxury apartments'. Each of those phrases has one of the words from your broad keyword – either 'luxury' or 'cars'. Neither are particularly targeted to 'luxury cars', though. The more untargeted your traffic, the less likely it is to convert.

Phrase match targeting will display your ad to people who type in the keyword phrase in addition to something else. For example, your 'luxury cars' ad could be shown to someone searching for 'second-hand luxury cars'. In this case, your exact keyword phrase appears in the search term, but if you don't sell second-hand luxury cars, it is again untargeted.

Exact match targeting will only display your ad to people who have typed in your specific search term exactly, with nothing else added.

Using exact match targeting, you'll have much more control over your ad spend and ensure that it's targeting the most qualified traffic.

Also, when advertising with Google AdWords, the ad placements are separated into two categories – 'search' and 'display'. The search ads are the ones that appear when people go to Google and type in a keyword phrase. The display ads are the ones that appear in banner slots in other websites. They represent two vastly different prospects.

The search prospect is someone who has specifically gone to Google and typed in what they're looking for. They are an active searcher (and possibly buyer). In comparison, the display prospect has simply seen your ad on some other website. They may have no immediate urgency for your offer. They may only be seeing it because there is some tenuous link between your ad and the page they're currently viewing. With all things being equal, the ad that converts a search prospect won't perform as well to a display prospect.

## How Product Format Affects Profitability

If you're selling products online, the most profitable types of products are typically digital products. They can be delivered to a single customer, or a thousand customers, without costing you any more aside from some additional hosting bandwidth. Even if you have physical products, the easiest way to increase profitability is to look at also providing them in a digital format.

For example, if you're selling a physical book via your website, could you instead offer that as a digital product? Set up a simple test to see which one generates more profit for you – the physical version or the digital version. You may find that you can sell the digital version at a lower price point while generating a higher profit. A lower price point will typically mean higher conversion rates, and therefore more customers too.

If you've got a $10 physical book, you may only make $3 profit per book after production and shipping costs. Sell that same book as a $7 digital version, and your profit is $7 (or perhaps minus a penny or two for bandwidth).

By lowering the price and changing the format, you've more than doubled your profit per unit sold. Most likely, you'll get more sales per 100 visitors with that lower price point too.

You're not restricted to just using one format either. Another option would be to keep your physical book as the main frontend offer, while giving people a second-chance 'exit popup' offer for the digital version.

Similarly, if you sell the digital version up front, you could offer people the physical version as a quick upsell/bump offer. Just have them pay shipping and handling. It can give you the best of both worlds. You get higher conversions from the digital offer, but also more people reading your physical copy, which will typically lead to higher consumption.

## Sequencing Your Products for Maximum Profitability

You might be promoting lots of different products, whether they're your own or products you're promoting as an affiliate. You'll find that not every promotion you do generates the same kind of results. Some promotions will outperform the average, and others will fall some way below it. A certain portion of your leads will unsubscribe with each email. Or they go cold and just stop responding to your messages, which is perfectly normal and expected.

For that reason, you want to ensure that all your leads are seeing the most profitable promotions first. To measure that, a good indicator is to assess the earnings per click (or alternatively, earnings per email). Measure it for each promotion and work out an average across all promotions. Then arrange them in your autoresponder follow-up sequence in order of descending EPC levels (as long as it makes sense to your customer's journey).

With a sequence of 10 different product promotions, the first one will be the promotion that yields the highest EPC. The last one will be that which yields the lowest. All your leads will see the best-performing promotion this way. If you put it at the back of the sequence, a lot fewer leads would see that offer because leads go cold or unsubscribe.

Similarly, if you're testing new promotions and affiliate offers, you should always be tracking their results. Any new, high-performing offers should be inserted into the sequence in the appropriate place, not just at the end.

## More Profit Without Selling More

Merchant accounts are an area where it's also possible to realize small gains that can add up to a significant amount over time. If you're selling online, then there are ways to both minimize your costs and increase your customer value, depending on what processing solution you use and how much volume you do.

A payment processor like Stripe will help reduce your churn rate with their automatic card updater. They work directly with card networks to keep customer card details up to date for you. That is a great way to increase the lifetime value of a customer.

Many people won't be inclined to sign up for a product again once their card expires and the billing stops. If the customer has to sign up all over again, they have to make that commitment again. If, however, their details are kept up to date, they don't have to make another commitment and will keep paying for at least a while longer. With a solution like this, you're virtually guaranteed to generate more profit per customer.

For customers who do want to cancel, have a representative on your team whose job is to try and save that sale. Sometimes a courtesy call from a real person is enough to get someone re-engaged or find out about any issues the customer may be having. Other times it could be as simple as the card owner not realizing the subscription was canceled when their card details changed. You won't save every sale. But by having someone reach out, you should be able to salvage revenue that would otherwise have been lost.

Customers looking to refund are another area in which you can attempt to save the sale. If you can halve your refund rate, you can get a significant boost in profitability.

When someone asks for a refund, you should obviously agree to that if it's your policy. But you can always ask them first if they would like a different product in exchange. Make the product in exchange be of greater value than their purchase, and the customer is more likely to agree.

Digital products cost you next to nothing to fulfill this way, other than the cost of having someone engage with the customer. Remember that it's much easier to get an existing customer to buy from you again than it is to generate a new customer. It's worth investing a little into keeping those customers happy.

Chargebacks are similar to refunds, with the exception that you typically can't communicate with the customer. They are equally as important, if not more so, as refunds. In fact, if your chargeback rate goes above 1% of transactions, then you could end up having issues with your merchant provider, where they place reserves on your account, or worse, close it completely.

The downside of chargebacks is that you don't just lose out on the sale revenue. You'll also be hit with a chargeback fee just for the privilege of someone filing one against you. A typical fee is around $25 per chargeback. That may not seem like a huge amount, but if you get a chargeback for a $10 sale, an extra $25 charge doesn't help your profitability in the slightest. Fighting a chargeback will also often require a significant investment of manpower to collate all the documentation for an appeal.

Unfortunately, a lot of people use chargebacks as a way to get their money back, even when not entitled to it. They know the card companies will side with them. Other people will just file one if they don't recognize the charge on their statement. Finally, there are those who will actively abuse the system in order to get 'free' stuff by purchasing it and then claiming they never authorized it.

The first step to minimizing the odds of that happening is to have very clear terms and conditions that people have to agree to. It's not enough to have a small link to your terms hidden at the bottom of your page. Have people enter their initials or electronically sign during the checkout. That will go a long way to proving the customer agreed to your terms.

It's also important to have your support details listed clearly on your page. Remind people they will see a charge on their account and tell them the identifier they will see there. Many card processors will allow you to customize the identifier that goes on the card statements. Use it to give more information to your customers.

You are restricted to just a few characters, so for my own business I put a very short web address there. People can type it in, and it will take them to a page that explains they purchased something from me. It explains who I am and how to get help or clarification on what they purchased. That measure will minimize claims from people who do not recognize the charge.

Finally, when it comes to payment processors, try to negotiate a lower fee. Many processors will give you a discount, particularly if you have a significant volume with them. Depending on the volume, you may be able to decrease your fees by more than 10% in relative terms. Going from 2.9% to 2.3% would be a relative 20% decrease in fees.

It's also worth considering how much international trade you do. Some processors will charge a higher rate for international transactions (currently PayPal charges US businesses 2.9% for US sales, but 3.9% for international sales).

In this case, it may be worth setting up an international business to collect the international sales. Just make sure the savings in fees will offset any administrative costs associated with the international company.

If dealing with foreign currency, deposit in a bank using local currency first. Then use a service like TransferWise to transfer revenue, as opposed to letting your processor convert to another currency. Typically, there will be a 2-3% spread on the exchange rate that you will incur by letting your payment provider convert the funds.

When it comes to spending money in your business, consider using a credit card that offers a cashback facility. Many of those cards will give you from 1% to 2% back on any purchases you make. The more you use the card, the more you're cutting costs overall in your business. It should go without saying that to get the benefit of this cashback, you need to pay off the balance before the interest payments kick in.

Even though the amounts may be relatively small, it's the combined effect of finding lots of these small changes that adds up to significant results.

## Streamlining Your Support

Providing support for your customers is an expense. There are usually ways to make the support more efficient. Ask yourself whether you really need to have someone manning the support desk, or the phone lines, all the time. Analyze when you get most of your support queries and plan your staff hours around those times.

Minimize the amount of support you have to provide by ensuring you have an in-depth knowledge base or FAQ section on your site. People can get answers to the most common questions without the need to submit a ticket or call the helpline.

Having someone manning the phones for eight hours a day, dealing with 80% of the same queries, is not efficient. Streamline the support by providing a knowledge base, and then have someone spend an hour a day answering any tickets that come through. That way, they have an hour of focused time to get the same results as someone spending eight hours of sporadic work.

Another, perhaps more controversial, way to cut down on your support load is to fire problem customers. They say the customer is always right. Honestly, if you've been in business any length of time, you know there are some people you just can't please.

Some customers will constantly complain, regardless of what you do. Others will badmouth your company, even when you go above and beyond for them. Fire them.

Customers most likely to fit into this category are the ones who spend the least amount with you but expect the most in return. If a customer has only spent ten or twenty dollars with you, but is taking up hours and hours of support time, it doesn't take long for them to cost you money to be a customer.

## Dropping Excess Weight From Your Business

You probably subscribe to lots of tools and services for your business. Many of them, such as hosting and autoresponders, are what I would class as essential. But there are lots of other services you can do without.

Every six months or so, I go through all my pre-existing payment agreements to find out what I'm currently paying for. Then I assess whether or not it's worth keeping it.

Many times, it's not that a tool doesn't work as it was supposed to, but that I didn't use it as much as I originally thought. Or perhaps there's a newer tool with similar (or even better) capabilities that I might use instead. Cut out the things you can do without, and you'll instantly be left with more profit at the end of each month.

It's important to note that the whole idea of being efficient in your business here is about cutting waste. However, it's one part of a larger process, and you can only improve profitability to a point. You cannot cut your way to growth. Your long-term goal should always be selling more, creating new offers, and generating new customers. These cuts should be used to make a profitable business more profitable; not to turn a failing business around just by cutting costs.

# Chapter 9

# AUTOMATION

This topic is probably one of my favorites. It's the one I devote a lot of my time to in both my own business and for clients I work with. Your goal should be to automate whatever you can so it frees you up to grow your business and not just work in it.

For me personally, automation is not all about making more money, but also about making more freedom. My business is a means to an end, in that it gives me the freedom to spend time with my family, work from home, and watch my sons grow up. However, it doesn't matter what you do with that free time. You may want to have more personal free time or do more in your business. The goal should be to have the freedom to choose how you spend your time rather than being a slave to your business.

Today, my business is built around automated sequences, and these sequences are responsible for most of the revenue in my business. It wasn't always that way, but over time I've been able to analyze the different elements and automate where possible. The rewards are incredible.

## Selling in Your Sleep

To give an example from my own business, I'm a big fan of using automated webinars to sell products and services online, particularly higher-priced products. Webinars work well because you get to present to an audience that is actively engaged with you and paying attention to you. That is something you can't achieve with a more passive sales message, such as a sales page or even a video sales letter. Prospects can pause the video, leave the page, check Facebook, or just not pay attention.

Most webinars require you as the product owner to be physically on the line to present the information, and many people reading this have probably attended such webinars before. You'll know how you can engage with the presenter, ask them questions, and sometimes get a personal response on the call.

For me, there are limitations to the live webinar model, simply because my target audience is mostly based in North America, while I currently live in the UK. With the time difference, I would have to stay up until 3 - 4 a.m. to present a webinar at the ideal time for a North American audience. My business is all about generating more freedom for myself, and staying up until 4 a.m. to sell a product on a webinar isn't my idea of freedom.

I also don't like presenting the same thing over and over again to different audiences. It's just not at all efficient. That's why I predominantly use automated webinars which run 24 hours a day, every day of the week, even when I'm asleep.

Trust me, it's incredibly satisfying to wake up in the morning seeing that four to five figures in sales have come in overnight from those automated webinars. I know it's an entirely overused cliché to claim you make money in your sleep, but with an automated webinar you really can.

The key to getting automated webinars to work well is to ensure that they simulate a live event as closely as possible. Live webinars work so well because they're live events where people give you their attention for 60 minutes or so. To be successful with automated webinars, you need to create that same sensation for the user. It should be said that you don't want to mislead people and claim the webinar is live if it's not. But if you set it up correctly, most people would not be able to tell the difference between a live webinar and an automated one.

One thing to note about automated webinars is that you typically won't get conversion rates as high as a live event. The technology has improved so that in many cases you can't tell if the video feed is live or pre-recorded. But the one main difference between the two is that on a live webinar the presenter can interact with specific attendees. That's just not possible with automated webinars. There's no way to address someone by their first name and answer the unique question they may have typed in. You can still have someone on your team manually replying to the chat via the messaging function. Though obviously, that's still not quite the same as the presenter reading out your question, addressing you by name, and then replying to you personally on the call.

With that said, you shouldn't be put off by that. The extra free time you get can be worth a lot more than the drop-off in conversions. For one of my webinars, I had over 25,000 people view the automated version. It took me two hours to record the webinar. I obviously had to prepare the presentation and the slides, but that was something I would have to do for a live event anyway.

Preparing for it didn't take me any longer than for a live event.

Assuming I could get an average 100 people onto a live webinar each time, I would need to run 250 live webinars to reach the same 25,000 people. At two hours per webinar, that's 500 hours I would have to spend doing live webinars. Compare that to just two hours for recording the automated version one time.

Consider the average work year consists of around 2,000 hours, and it means I'd have to spend three months of work just presenting webinars if I chose to do them live. Plus, given the time zone difference between where I live and where my audience live, all those webinars would be in the middle of the night. By using an automated webinar, I had 'found' an extra three months of time. I could spend that doing more productive things in my business. Imagine how much three months would be worth to you.

Even though they may convert less than a live webinar, they don't convert *much* less than a live version. Certainly not so much less that it would be better for me to spend 250 nights doing them live.

Another problem with live webinars is that you only make sales when you're doing them. If you can't present them, you can't sell with them. With an automated webinar, it doesn't matter if I'm traveling, or just taking the day off to spend with my kids. The webinars will still run and possibly generate sales.

An automated webinar also gives you the ability to reach people in their own time zone with a timing that suits their schedule. While the bulk of my customers may be based in North America, there are also customers in Europe, Australia, and many other countries too. For most people in those other countries, it would be impractical to attend a session that's targeted to a US audience.

The only solution for a live webinar would be doing multiple webinars to cater for different time zones. That's creating more work, not less.

With the automated webinar, prospects can choose the best day, and best time of day, for them. That will in turn give you a much higher opt-in rate from your registration page.

If you drive people to a page and they know they won't be able to attend, they won't register. However, if you provide them with a choice of times in their time zone, they're more likely to register. Even if they don't attend, you can follow up with them. In many cases, the increased opt-in rate you get from having more flexible times can offset any decrease in sales conversions from not having an actual live event.

One advantage that automated webinars have over a live one is the ability to run effective split tests. When you're using live webinars, you can't do that because every audience is different. Every presentation you do is slightly different too, even if it's just down to certain tones you use, certain questions you answer on the call, etc. With an automated webinar, the exact same video is presented to each attendee. You can run split tests on elements of the process, knowing that there are no other variables at play in your test other than the ones you define.

If there was one thing I could recommend to people that would have the biggest impact in their business, it would be to create a product you can sell for a minimum of $1,000, set up with an automated webinar, and drive targeted traffic to. Add in some evergreen scarcity to the promotion, and you'll be unstoppable.

## Automating Other Aspects

Beyond automated webinars, your email marketing can be fully automated as well. I've shown the benefits of creating a follow-up sequence in your autoresponder, but the real gains come from creating evergreen launch sequences.

You may be familiar with the product-launch-style sequence. With that sequence, someone will mail out several pieces of pre-launch content, then open up a cart to sell a product for a limited time. Finally, they'll close down the offer so that it is no longer available after a certain date.

That method works extremely well. One of the main reasons it does so is the scarcity built in around the hard deadline. A lot of people would just run this launch sequence once or maybe twice a year. It's actually possible to run it 365 days a year by using a follow-up sequence with evergreen scarcity built in for each lead.

The way it works is that every single lead that enters your funnel will receive the exact same sequence, but the links and deadlines for the individual subscriber are unique and dynamically generated.

If Bob joins your list on a Monday, his sequence may end with a hard deadline on a Monday two weeks later.

If Jenny joins on a Wednesday, she would go through the exact same sequence as Bob, but with her hard deadline being on Wednesday two weeks later.

Compare that to running a launch once, or even twice, a year. You will get much better results.

With the automated sequence, 100% of your leads will go through that process. If you're waiting six months between ruining a 'live' launch, a large portion of those leads will have unsubscribed, gone cold, or just stopped opening your emails completely. If you only do the launch once a year, even fewer leads will see your launch sequence.

When someone enters your funnel, they're a hot prospect looking for a solution. Even if you can get them to open your emails six or twelve months later, there's no guarantee they will still have that same need. With an automated email sequence, you can get all the benefits of a live launch, but ensure that the maximum amount of people see that offer. Moreover, you're providing them with a solution while they are still a hot prospect.

You can also combine it with an annual live launch if you wish. You simply close down the 'live' page and put up a waiting list opt-in form. When people enter their name for the waiting list, use an automated sequence that gives them a limited window to get access to the course. Again, the expiration date is unique for each subscriber based on when they opt in to that page.

Beyond this, it's likely that you'll continue to do some broadcast promotions to your list. Any offers that do particularly well can be converted to run in an evergreen format and added to your follow-up sequence. String a few of these together in your follow-up sequence, and you'll have something that's working to drive sales for you every single day of the year.

## Chapter 10

# DELEGATION

Finally, we're onto a section I know a lot of business owners struggle with: giving responsibility to other people and delegating tasks in their business. The goal with delegating is to free up more of your time to grow your business. That way, your time is always spent on the most profitable activities. While automation can help you leverage your time efficiently, there are inevitably tasks that need to be handled by a real person. But that person doesn't have to be you.

You might have resisted outsourcing or delegating work so far. It's important to consider that if you're doing everything yourself, each task costs you the same as an hourly rate. Whether that be dealing with customer support, keeping the books up to date, creating products, or building strategic relationships with affiliates and partners. You'll find that some of those tasks are a lot more profitable than others. As the business owner, you should be focusing on the highest-level, most profitable tasks.

Product creation is always a task that has a high profitability factor, more so than you may realize.

Let's assume you can create a product that will generate $100,000 in revenue, and it takes you a total of 100 hours to put it together. Your hourly rate for working on that product is $1,000 an hour.

If you make a product that can generate that amount per year, with a shelf life of at least five years, then your hourly rate for that product creation goes up to $5,000 an hour.

Compare that to doing customer support yourself. There is no way you will be able to generate that kind of hourly rate from answering customer emails and phone calls. While good customer service will ultimately help to build a relationship with customers, you can do that just as easily with a trained team who you may be paying $20-$30 per hour.

## How to Figure Out What to Delegate First

The easiest way to figure out what you should be outsourcing first is to make a list of all the tasks you're currently doing. Then you need to assign a value to those tasks.

Simply take the revenue you generate per year (or per month) and divide it by the number of hours you work in that same time period.

If you pay yourself $100,000 per year, and you're working 40 hours a week for 50 weeks of the year, then your hourly rate is $50.

With your hourly rate and the list of all your tasks, ask yourself which of those tasks you could outsource for less than your hourly rate. Taking the example above, any task that can be outsourced for less than $50 should be delegated to someone else.

It's important to note that the hourly rate is based on the average of all your time spent. There will be tasks that are $10/hour tasks and others that are $1,000/hour tasks. When you free up time by outsourcing, you gain more than just the simple savings in your average hourly rate. It frees you up to focus on the higher-value tasks which earn you more.

For example, let's assume you have a $50 hourly rate and spend 10 hours a week on customer support. That's a cost of $500 per week to you. If you can outsource those 10 hours a week at $25 per hour, then you are saving $250.

But what is really happening is that you're saving 10 hours a week to focus on high-earning tasks.

Now you can dedicate those 10 free hours to product creation. If you know your hourly rate for product creation is $1,000 per hour, you've added an extra $10,000 in potential revenue. That's a lot more than just the $250 savings based on an average hourly rate. That is why it's key you understand the value of each of the tasks in your business.

Sometimes you may feel like you're the only person who can do the task at 100%, and that nobody else will ever be able to achieve the same level in their work. It's still best to outsource it. Someone who can do the job 80-90% as well as you still leaves you with that time to focus on more important tasks. Those tasks are where you can deliver 100% yourself. Having a team of people all operating at 80% is a lot more productive than doing everything yourself at 100%.

One of the unexpected benefits I've encountered from having a team is that they will see things from a different point of view to me. In cases where I feel like I'm the only one who can do something the right way, a team member has actually pointed out a more efficient way of doing it that I had completely missed. As a result, I'm not only delegating that task, but now that task is done in a much more efficient way. If I'd not attempted to find someone else to do that task, I'd still be doing it myself, the slow way.

I also recommend you spend some time paying attention to everything you're doing in your business. If you find there are things you're repeating, then either record yourself doing them or create a quick document that outlines those steps. Anything you do more than three times is something that can probably be outsourced to someone else (if not automated).

As you build up a list of processes, you'll be able to give it to anyone who joins your team. They'll have an almost 'paint by numbers' approach to the tasks they need to accomplish. While it may take you a small investment in time to create those documents, it's worth it. You'll be able to use them over and over again for each new team member you bring on board.

## Letting Go

It can be difficult to put that trust in other people at first, so start small if you're struggling to let go. Things like customer support, administrative work, accounting, and those types of tasks are easily handled by someone else. More often than not, they're not particularly fun tasks, so you shouldn't miss them too much.

In fact, if there's something you don't enjoy, it's often better to find someone who can do it for you. If you don't enjoy it, you procrastinate and spend more time on it. It's better to pay someone just to get it done. That leaves you with freedom to focus on tasks you do enjoy.

There are lots of tasks you can do yourself that are better outsourced to a professional, even if you enjoy doing them. A prime example is getting your sales copy created. You may enjoy writing sales copy, and even be moderately accomplished. But you're not as good as a professional who's been studying the subject for years and has made a career out of it. Even though copywriters can be expensive, it can cost you money in the long run to not pay for professional copy.

Let's say you can write a sales letter that converts at 1%. A professional could get 1.5%, but it costs $5,000 to hire them. That's a conservative estimate. In most cases, I would estimate a professional could at least double the conversions of what an average business owner could achieve.

With those numbers, it means if you were able to generate $10,000 in sales from a certain amount of traffic, then the professional copy would have generated $15,000 in sales. Take off the fee for the copy, and the net profit is the same at $10,000.

There is no difference at this point in overall profit. However, for every sale going forward, it costs you money not to use the professional sales copy.

If that product with your DIY copy goes on to sell $100,000 worth of product, the professional copy would have sold $150,000.

Subtract the $5,000 fee for the copy, and you would still have made an extra $45,000 with the professional copy.

Good sales copy is not an expense but an investment. It's the very thing that will make the difference between someone getting their credit card out or not. You should always be looking to present the most persuasive copy possible to your prospects. In the long run, it will be more than worth it.

The same can be said for other aspects of your business and in relation to hiring consultants or coaches to help you grow. While you may be able to figure some things out yourself, a coach that has already "been there and done that" will help you get results faster. They'll also help avoid mistakes that can cost you a significant amount of time or money.

You may be able to get some results going it on your own, but the results you get from hiring a coach and leveraging their expertise will likely be substantially better.

Another factor to consider when hiring someone is the opportunity cost of doing it all yourself. If it takes a longer time to get the same result, that's time wasted. Even if you could write persuasive sales copy, but it takes you 20 hours of work to do so, that's 20 hours you could be spending on other tasks. Don't be afraid to invest money in experts who can help you get better results and also free up more time.

# CONCLUSION AND NEXT STEPS

You made it! You have finished this book, so you now have a proven blueprint for at least doubling your business by focusing on small changes. This is the same blueprint I follow when building out campaigns for myself and clients that go on to generate seven figures or more.

Right now, you might be feeling a little like a deer in the headlights, not sure which way to go. That's understandable, as you've just digested a lot of information. It's easy to get paralyzed from information overload.

My goal with this book is to show you how to break down big goals (e.g. doubling your business) into smaller, more achievable steps (e.g. just 10% improvement in one area).

You don't need to try to do everything in this book all at once, but you do need to do something. Start small and build on that.

You can easily take each chapter of this book in isolation and focus solely on that. It might take you a whole month to get a 10% improvement in that one section. But by the end of eight months, you will have doubled your business. Not bad, right?

And if you don't already have a business, the extra reports at the link below will give you some ideas on how to start building a business the right way.

If you haven't already done so, make sure to grab those bonuses from:

www.SevenFigureBlueprints.com/bonuses

It's important to note that the journey doesn't have to end at simply doubling your business. The fact that you were able to find a 10% improvement should show you that you can find even more improvements.

There is always a way to improve. Some areas may lend themselves to larger gains, but don't forget that any gain is still a gain. All gains take you one step closer to your goal. The key is to keep moving forward and have faith in the process. If you do that, the results may surprise you.

Imagine if Sir Dave Brailsford had told the cyclists on his team they would win the Tour de France just by washing their hands better. They would have laughed at him. But that was just one tiny part of the process. The power is in the cumulative effects of all the little things you do each day to improve, no matter how small.

One of the things I love about this process is that it can have such a dramatic effect – not only on someone's business, but on their lives as a whole.

It's immensely satisfying for me to help people make a difference in the world.

Originally, I wrote this book as a way to share my process and help as many people as I could. I also know it's impossible to put everything I know into just one book, particularly when there are so many different types of businesses and products.

If you're keen to start implementing this process but aren't sure of the best way to move forward, or simply want to fast-track your success, I do work with a small number of businesses in a hands-on fashion. If that's something you would benefit from, reach out and let's talk here:

www.SevenFigureBlueprints.com/talk

With that, I just want to say thanks for reading this book and good luck!

Richard Legg

www.ingramcontent.com/pod-product-compliance
Lightning Source LLC
Chambersburg PA
CBHW021425180326
41458CB00001B/137
* 9 7 8 1 9 9 9 7 3 8 8 3 9 *